Find Yourself

Go the Distance to Discover Your Meaning

SYLVIA SALOW

For every beautiful soul who has been through darkness and is longing to come home – back to their true selves.

CONTENTS

ACKNOWLEDGMENTS

I am the most grateful for my husband, who has always believed in me and supported my life calling. You always inspire me to step into my greatness.

I would like to thank every soul who has ever helped me to find myself. Beginning from the strangers, I have only met briefly to those who have joined me on my life path.

My thanks also go to the many friends I met in China. Ivan, I know that we will never forget our first talk on a plane to Hong Kong. I want to also thank Caren, Hana, Jeanette, Damon, Gregory, Emmanuel, Piccolo, Lai, and others.

I also want to take a moment to acknowledge my grandparents, who were a harbor of love and support throughout most of my life. Although our contact was not as frequent as I wished, you were always in my heart. Thank you for all the lessons you taught me.

I thank my kindred spirit, my sister, for accompanying me on my path since I was 10 years old.

My thanks also belong to Kahl, who has acted as the greatest catalyst for my spiritual growth and who set me on the path I now so gladly walk.

My big thanks belong to the city of Xiamen for taking care of me and offering me a home when I needed it the most.

PREFACE

Little did I know where my search for my true self would take me. In our world, we need to travel the distance to uncover who we are independent of the demands of our society.

Finding your true self is both an act of recreating and remembrance. When you begin to remember who you once used to be, you remove your false identities and recreate yourself from the ashes of your previous existence. On my search to find myself, I have discovered that everyone has a divine blueprint carrying the unique substance of their true essence. Our innate nature is unaffected by anything in this world, yet each of our experiences guides our spirit to express itself in unique ways.

When you live by a polluted river, at some point, you feel thirsty for clean water. You are done with the trash other people throw down the river, so you begin a journey upstream toward the clear spring. Without a map or an idea about how far you need to travel to find the spring, your steps are propelled by the desire in your heart. Day after day, you set off for yet another leg of your journey.

The journey leads you to unexpected places; deserts, deep valleys, mountains, and still you continue because the closer you get, the stronger faith you cherish in your heart. It must be somewhere near you reassure yourself while stepping on loose stones along a steep cliff. The Earth itself under your feet guides you with determination and love toward your next destination. Sometimes you sit down in exhaustion and question the worth of your journey. Other times you joyfully frolic because you can hear the silent roar of the spring within your heart. While traversing through different territories, you need to summon your inner strength.

Without you noticing it, every step recreates you again and again. The pilgrimage challenges you to take off one piece of your personality, for you cannot carry your anger to the peaks of the highest mountains. The intensity of your wrath would mislead your steps. Neither can you delve in your sadness because its heaviness would take you back to the familiar place down the river where everyone else continued to live. As you peel off the layers of who you are not anymore, you begin to feel something new yet something intimate.

In the darkest of nights of your odyssey, you spot something unusual - a little light is guiding you. Now it is not as dark as during the first nights, and the little light fills you with hope. Your mind naturally guides you to search for the source of the light. You look around yourself to see whether someone else walks beside you. As you narrow your eyes, you catch a glimpse of a shadow. Perhaps there is a person who is the source of the little light. Your heart jumps joyfully as you continue searching for that shadow to see the kind soul guiding you through the night. As days pass, your mind convinces you that the person must truly love you to accompany you through this unknown territory. Then the morning comes, and you feel refreshed with new hope that not only you are coming closer to the spring, but you also have found love along the way.

In the following couple of weeks, your eyes pursue the shadow of the person walking beside you. The person is so near, so close that you could almost touch them, yet so far that you have never seen their real face. One night, the hope begins to die within you; maybe the person is not real.

Perhaps they do not love you. Then you hear a loving voice, "What if the person was not the source of the little light?" Even though you do not know who said it, it rekindles joy within your heart. In that sudden realization, you know that you do not need someone else to walk beside you because you will arrive regardless. It is your voyage, after all.

The next night, your mind is excited about a wonderful idea to look for a different source of the little light. "What could it be?" You keep asking yourself. Then you lift your head and look up to the skies. "Oh, stars! Of course!" You are beyond excited to discover the real source of the light. Now you do not mind when the night arrives because you know that the stars will guide you. Each night your connection to stars grows stronger. "If only I could be up there among the stars, then all my problems would vanish. Perhaps I would not need to find the spring anymore." Sometimes your love for the stars undermines your determination. A slight dissatisfaction arises in your heart; maybe you do not want to be on this odyssey after all. Could it be that you belong among the stars?

Instead of finding relief in the stars, a sense of detachment from your journey slowly spreads in your heart. Your steps feel heavier than ever before. You feel lonelier because it seems that the place you belong could never inhabit the same space as you. Now you feel utterly alone. You left everyone you know behind, and you realize that you cannot return to the polluted river anymore. You have come so far. How could you go back to your old life now? It was only an illusion that the waters of your life were meant to be dirty. Now, you already know that you can lessen the distance between you and the source.

The brave person, whose shadow you saw, was conceivably a result of your imagination. What a hopeful thought to believe that someone else would walk this path with you! What a silly belief that they could even love you! No, everything transpired in your own mind. In all your loneliness, the nights grow darker as you turn your eyes away from the stars. What is the point of looking up to them if you can never reach them?

Now you walk alone in the cold mountains without a shelter. Everything that you loved is gone. Merely the flesh of your body and the incessantly chattering voice in your head are now accompanying you. Your legs feel heavy, sometimes even unable to move. When you lay your body to rest, you dream of a better world. It must be out there! But where? Will you ever find it? What if the whole pilgrimage is only a fantasy? But what can you do now that you have come so far? In despair, you realize that there is nowhere to return. As you have wandered, you witnessed that every bridge burnt down to the ashes after you crossed it. If you jumped in the river, its mighty stream would tear you apart. "No, there is no turning back," you whisper.

In the morning, you recommit to continue, but the joy has vacated your body. You feel empty. The old you is gone, but the new you has not arrived yet. "Who am I, now, when everything I used to be is gone?" You look at your reflection in the river, but you do not recognize your face anymore. The features of your face are sharper, and your eyes are piercing. "Who am I becoming?" The gaze in your eyes reminds you of something, but the remembrance seems so distant. You turn your sight away when suddenly you hear that loving voice again, "Remember, remember."

"Who is it talking to me?" It cannot be your ego, which is like a commander spitting out one order and hurtful sentence after another. But what is it? Where have you heard this voice before? You look back at your reflection, and you notice your lips involuntarily whispering, "Remember, remember, remember."

"Who am I?" you ask yourself once again. Out of the blue, you sense the presence of something new. It vibrates in every cell of your body, and you allow it to take over you. It is like a warm liquid light spreading in your body and radiating all around you. You are enveloped by a cloud of tenderness, and it feels like your true home. Your origin. "Is this what I have always been looking for? Perhaps it is not up in the stars! Maybe my origin is within me. But where?" you ask.

The ecstatic sensation grows stronger as if your questions spur its intensity. One moment, it feels overwhelming, yet a moment later, it feels like you have always been this strong. An unknown strength emerges from this loving sensation. It brings certainty and clarity, as well as infinite love. "What is this love that is so powerful, so strong?" you enquire.

As you speak those words, something guides your attention to the center of your chest. You close your eyes to feel its presence. The powerful love intensifies as if it desires to gush out from your body, so you allow it. Now you experience the most extraordinary sensation of bliss that you have ever felt. And immediately, you know beyond all doubt that this love can change the world. It feels powerful beyond measure and yet loving and tender at the same time. In your heart, you look equally at everything alive that surrounds you. That love penetrates everything like nuclear energy. In the presence of that love, nothing has a chance to remain the same. Neither do you.

A different power that you had never witnessed before was born within you. It does not try to possess anything, and yet it is ever-present. This love does not worship material possessions or people, and yet it loves everything and everyone with the same magnitude. That power does not deprive others of their freedom; it liberates them from the bondage of illusions. It restores their vision and awakens the same power within themselves. In the presence of this love, everyone has their place in this world and their own uniqueness that yearns to be born. This new yet familiar love does not compete; it encompasses everyone and everything.

"Is this what I have been looking for my whole life?" you cannot help but ask. And in your heart, you recognize the answer, you have always known it. It was the presence of this powerful love that guided you to remember. That little loving voice that you could only hear in the most desperate of moments. Now nothing outside yourself seems alluring, and yet it gains new glow. How could you have forgotten this love when it has been perfectly hidden within you all along?

You have walked the distance to find it, you have searched every nook and cranny, and yet that loving power has incessantly guided you from within yourself. You have hunted for it in another person. You have explored the Earth and the stars to find that little something, so fragile and yet so powerful, while every step of your journey has conspired to awaken the loving presence within your heart. Now, you know who you are, and for the first time, you also recognize the true essence of others. When you look at them, you do not see the flesh. You feel their powerful, loving presence, and you help them to remember it too.

The morning comes, and you are ecstatic to notice that the spring is right in front of you. At last, you have arrived. It has been a long search, longer than you could have imagined. Along the path, you have been tested and initiated into yet new realms within your true self. As you put aside one illusionary thought after another, you did something essential; you have emptied yourself of the strings of your old personality.

Back there down the river, people tried to convince you that you are just like them. Now you know that they were right, yet they did not know their true selves. What unites you is that loving power flowing from your heart and through your body, not your achievements, status, or how well you fit in the society. You needed to travel the distance to recognize that.

When your lips taste the first sips of the pure water, you know why you needed to undertake that journey. Only a few dare to travel to this place entirely hidden in the mountains, yet it is our true origin. As you lay your body on the grass, you begin to remember that once upon a time, you lived in this sacred space. Once, it was your home where you were safe and beloved.

A stream of memories surfaces, and although you cannot sharpen your sight well enough to capture their meaning, your heart knows, you have found the place where you belong. You have arrived. Yet this time you are different than when you first abandoned this beautiful space, the pilgrimage has changed you. You are a transformed being. As your legs carried you toward the spring, you have traveled through different landscapes, and which have all revealed something fundamental about who you are.

As you sip more of the fresh waters of your new home, you realize that it is this loving presence that also connects you with the stars. After all, you are not alone and forsaken here on Earth. You carry the stars within your heart. "How can I feel more of your presence?" you ask the stars. As if your question held another key to the mysterious door, the loving presence within your heart grows further and reaches for the stars. With your inner eye, you can observe a white light approaching you. Once again, you hear the words, "Remember, remember who you truly are."

You open your arms to welcome the white light and let it gently enter your body. It traveled from the stars down to Earth, and now it is within you. "What is this light?" you ponder out loud. At that moment, the answer arrives. "Of course! It is my soul!"

Before you embarked on your quest, you had not realized how much you missed the connection with your soul. You assumed that "soul" was merely a cute term for some indescribable metaphysical concept. Except now it dwells in your body. It is not a theory for you anymore - you have embodied your soul. This is your true essence; your real self. You are all of it; the Earth, the body, the stars, the heart, the divine, and even your mind. No separation resides within all those aspects of yourself. As if the loving presence drew back together all the parts of you that you had cut off. How could you have known your true self when you were not whole?

In the nightmare of separation, you sought the answers in every disconnected part of your body. One after another, you kept them dearly in your hands and examined their tiniest aspects. As you held onto those parts, you assumed, "This must be me. No, this is me. No, it is this and that. But how come that I am still unhappy? Unsatisfied because of something that I cannot even find the words for?"

To mend those pieces together, you needed to embark on the transformational journey. Usually, we do not ask the universe to send us away from our homes. When the time arrives to take the first steps, we do not jump in excitement, and of course, we never feel ready. It is always lousy timing to search for the meaning behind the disturbing situations we encounter. For they agitate the eons of our long slumber. As we are caught up in the fascination of the shiny objects in our dream, we believe that the dream is the reality. But this unpleasant knocking on the door does not go away. We do not want to open our eyes and see what we could find behind the door. We are sure it cannot be more thrilling than our enchantment with relationships, money, appearance, or careers.

"No, go away," we mutter from our dream. We cannot open our eyes because there is another exciting pursuit to follow. Maybe it is another potential partner, "Oh, that excitement when it is new," we joyfully purr. Or the new quest can take the form of friends we know are wrong for us, but at least we feel accepted by them. Perhaps it is not the right time to open our eyes because now we need to earn a lot of money so we can travel or purchase a house.

The wake-up call never comes at the right moment. So what does the universe do? It takes on one of the pursuits of our dream and let it disintegrate in front of our eyes. Now our body trembles in shock and fury, "What has just happened?" We believe that we need to go to look for a replacement, and so we begin the inner transformation journey that eventually leads us upstream to our true self. As we walk, we purify ourselves of every false idea about who we are, or otherwise, our hearts would not have the space to hold the powerful, loving presence in our bodies. The time comes when we have to decide – will I go back to sleep, or do I continue my quest without even knowing what I am searching for?

Only brave souls reawaken that power within themselves. Yet everyone can choose to be courageous. Before the journey, no one has the map, and not a single soul knows what creatures they will encounter along the way. Yet, after the first steps, your willingness to see the new world and to stand in your real power starts to overweigh your fears. That willingness is enough because as long as you have it, you will always arrive.

Whatever distance you need to travel, know that you are not alone. Many people feel the disturbing call to wake up. One by one, we ignite that loving power within ourselves, and it guides us to our origin. Many have walked this sacred path of recreating and remembering their true selves before you, and many will follow. It is alright that it sometimes scares you. It is perfect that it is a messy, tiring journey, but bear in mind that every part of the journey always brings you closer toward your true essence.

Your essence is fabricated from the stardust lace and earthly soil. As you wander, you call in your soul closer until one day it merges with your body. This is the sacred union that will never allow you to fall back to sleep again. Your soul is the higher aspect of you, which is untouched by the heaviness of your body and by the eons of journeys in the realms of matter. Eventually, it will penetrate your body, emotions, and mind. When this happens, you bring heaven to earth. The marriage of soul and flesh is not about one thing being sacred and spiritual, while something else is material and ugly. The holy union spiritualizes and uplifts even the darkest dimensions within your heart and mind, and also the entirety of your human life. You do not need to reach out to stars; they draw closer to you. The bridge is completed.

This book is about building the bridge that leads you to your true self without even knowing where to begin or what your true self means. As your eyes sink onto the following pages, you will witness my transformational journey; my search for the clear spring up in the mountains. I invite you to see the depths of my heart, mind, and soul so that you recognize the steppingstones of your own journey of transformation as well. I will share with you my darkest moments as well as realizations that led me to encounter my soul and how this connection has changed my life. Although you are reading about my journey, the journey is yours, as well.

After hearing hundreds of stories from people all around the world, I cannot be deaf to the reality that there is a higher power reorganizing our lives at these crucial times in history. Although the details of everyone's transformation differ, we move through similar threads and stages that lead us to the same result – to become an embodied soul and to let the powerful presence of love to change our lives. That will eventually also spark a global transformation.

The disturbing wake-up calls of my journey have always come in the form of love. I have been seeking for that love from the early days through painful relationships to toxic friendships and all the way to meeting my twin flame. After I have looked within all those places, I have found the real source of the little light that has guided me all along.

Will you join me on this journey?

May this book show you the way.

May it heal your heart.

May it awaken the loving presence within you.

May you remember your true origin.

My heart is with you.

CHAPTER 1

ORIGIN

May all the stars unite in one!
Let my light shine again.
Be the hope, be the spark,
Let go of the fear to speak your love.

All the powers that come from within,
I call you once again to help me thrive.
Once, I was the shining star,
But now, the dust has covered my eyes.

What a pang of sadness, what a sorrow!
Your tears outshone your smile.
Who are you, the child of the Sun,
To get lost in your earthly life?

To whom you shine?
To whom you speak?
To wisdom?
Or to a silly belief?

Call back your beauty!
Remember your strength!
Embrace your purity once again!
You, the child of the Sun.

In many cultures, it is of the highest importance to know

and cherish your ancestors. I never understood why it mattered until I learned about family patterns. Knowing your origin is not only about the veneration of ancestors as an act of respect and honor, but it is also the path to find yourself. You cannot deny the place you come from. It defines you.

When you know your origin, you have a good starting point in life that offers you a solid foundation for the future. It provides you with firm roots so that nothing easily shakes you off your course. If you have a healthy family that supports you, you will blossom like a beautiful orchid that has all the sunlight and raindrops it needs. You have a sound bedrock, and thus you are better equipped to embrace life. Your family roots hold the sacred space for your lifelong expansion.

However, not everyone has received the loving support of their family. Lack of the initial grounding in life may break you if you allow it to happen. If your family does not support you and you do not feel loved, you grow up with self-doubts and insecurities. Instead of having a fresh start in life, you feel broken inside. Perhaps you feel anger and resentment to love. Or maybe you are more like I was, and you feel like something is wrong with you. You may not understand what is wrong, but still, it haunts you wherever you go. For some reason, you have not received the support your little soul desired. Now, you are out there on your own, and your mind incessantly tries to convince you that you do not deserve to be happy. Sooner or later, you begin to believe this little voice in your head, and you make choices that are rooted in fear. This is the breaking point when your story begins to determine you.

Still, wherever your origin is, it is vital to know your family and their life stories, which carry information that has made you the person you are. Their stories, hopes, and failures run in your veins and fabricate the deep-seated beliefs about what is possible for you. Everyone lets these beliefs to form their perception; it is inevitable. When we are little, we have no other reference point but our place of origin. Therefore we believe that our family and society are the perfect examples of what a healthy approach to life looks like. It takes growing up and a necessary dose of introspection to realize that it may not be the case.

My starting point was a tiny country in the heart of Europe. My journey began in a nation that was about to undergo a significant transition. When I was born, the former Czechoslovakia was still under the regime of the Soviet Union. It seemed symbolic to be born in a country going through a massive political change while my life was about to unfold through it. A mental, spiritual, and emotional transformation has always been a big theme in my life. Something deep within has always been urging me to evolve at a higher speed as if I would not have enough time to take it slow.

Growing up in a post-soviet country has allowed me to witness various aspects of the human mind and soul. During communism, people were suppressed, banned from speaking their truth, or doing anything that went against the Party. Unfortunately, this way of restricting the human spirit naturally led to the development of a firm resignation, apathy, and disappointment in people.

The Czech people have always been great inventors and artists. From inventing the arc lamp, laying the foundations for cellular biology, or to developing soft contact lenses, their imagination did not know limits. Yet, the reality of being ruled by Germans, Polish, and the Hapsburg monarchy for centuries eventually weakened the Czech spirit. The hearts of the Czech people have been wobbling from creativity to cynicism. From excitement to apathy. That was my heritage that I am now so grateful for. Though it took me a fair amount of inner growth to appreciate the set of cards I was given to play with - no accidents happen in the multi-layered, far beyond our understanding, universe. We carefully handpick the game settings, which motivate us, often through unpleasant experiences, to reach our potential. Or at least to expand the consciousness we were born with. The earlier we accept the cards we were endowed with, the sooner we learn to play the game of life.

When you fathom your origin, you decode the potential influences on your psyche. The origin is the roadmap for our unconscious acts, thoughts, feelings, and words. Thus we need to look beneath the surface to reveal the complex substances we are made of. Usually, we must be willing to see the uncomfortable and painful dynamics that have shaped our parents and grandparents. Since only then, we can actively participate in recreating ourselves based on who we truly are beneath the layers of conditioning.

The origin is not only about who our parents are or what our ancestors did. It is subtler forces that impact the human psyche. We do not only share similar genetics, but we also share identical conditioning of our minds. Whatever our parents and grandparents believed to be possible, we accepted it as our inherent limitations too. Their fears became our fears, and now they look real to us just like they seemed real to our parents. If our ancestors went through a trauma, our bodies still carry the same stress within our cells. Thus we should not only look at the obvious, but we should also understand the invisible because this is the key to our potential. When we do not change the setting of our minds, we recreate similar situations to what our parents did. It feels like we are unable to ever break through and be contented. Something within makes us sabotage our success, love, and happiness, and we become bitter and hopeless. It is the inside that needs to transform for life to mirror it back to us. We carry our origin in our minds, emotions, and bodies wherever we go.

Early on in my life, I could witness how the origin impacts people. I could understand how envy and jealousy break the human spirit or the myriad ways of how fear controls otherwise reasonable people. Unintentionally, I became an observer of life and studied the deepest motives behind people's decisions. At that time, I did not understand how this skill would become essential in my future. As a little girl, I also developed a well-refined sense to notice when people were misaligned with their hearts and souls. As soon as they entered the room, or my family mentioned the name of someone, I could feel dissonant frequencies emerging from their bodies. At that moment, I intuitively knew that that person was not genuine and was taking a detour from the path of their highest potential.

Another behavior that people seemed to be unaware of was being dishonest with themselves. Although I was used to the fact that most people lie to others, but I could not comprehend why they would also lie to themselves. I would see others unhappy in their relationships, their work, their school, and with themselves, yet they did not want to change it. On the contrary, they continued investing in their lives based on these little lies, and they kept reassuring themselves that everything was fine. Eventually, all the little lies would pile up and affect the rest of their lives.

It is an arduous task to attempt to find yourself if you do not dare to look at the depths of your heart and express what you find there. It took many years for me to realize that we cannot help other people if they do not want to change. Moreover, I understood that when something triggers us, we can use it as a fuel to change our own life. So I used the fuel of seeing unhappy people motivate me early on to find a way to feel happy, fulfilled, and peaceful. I used my pain points for my own inner expansion.

CHAPTER 2

THE DANCE OF ENERGIES

The world consists of light.
The frequencies are ever dancing,
Creating both day and night,
In their presence, I am blooming.

"See your touch through my eyes,
See the colors, hear the tones,"
This is the music of energies.
Hear the sound of their moans!

Take my hand, I will reveal to you whole existence!
Touch me with your heart and let the matter disappear.
Open your third eye to receive guidance.
Join us, the secret group of the ancient seers.

Energies weave a universal web together,
Conceiving the stars, the planets, and the suns.
You are made of sacred amber
From the race of the golden ones.

It was a warm evening of 2011, and I was gazing at the sunset when my thoughts led me to ponder about my roots and the hidden ways they have influenced my perception of life. A heavy mist lifted off my thinking the moment I realized how my past related to my present and future. The link had always been there, visible and right in front of my eyes. Yet while I was growing up, I did not allow myself to see it.

Often life needs to shake us in the most painful spot to make us finally listen. We must experience a deep inner turmoil before we start to seek the answers that had been haunting us for years. Some of my questions were, "Why do I feel sad almost every day? Why am I here on Earth? Who am I? Why did I have to suffer? Why could not my childhood be more loving? Why can my heart feel so much when it would be infinitely easier not to feel at all? Where am I going? What is the bigger picture of what is happening in my life right now?"

And then there came the most important question of all, "How can I live up to my potential?" Ever since I can remember, my potential has haunted me. It comes to me as visions, flashes of inspiration, feelings, and deep knowing that rush over my body. As if I watched a movie screen and observed the better version of myself. I can see the whole scene and fathom the significance of every step, but still, for most of my life, I remained an observer. This gap between me and my potential has always been overwhelming. Sometimes I wished that I would not be conscious of it every day.

Sensing your potential can be both motivating and crushing. As much as it instills you with hope and directs your steps, it also weighs you down because you know that you are not there yet. And the distance between you and your potential feels too far to travel. Especially if your origin did not provide you with the ideal starting point in life. A heavy burden weighed me down when I recognized that before I can make a move to my future destination, I needed to mend my past. I had to rewrite my history in a way that would elate me and make me stronger rather than break my wings. So, there I was, after the most painful year of my life, I had one of the hardest tasks ahead – to heal my relationship with my past.

By then, I already deciphered some dynamics of family patterns. As I slowly began to connect with my old suppressed emotions, a link between past situations and my present became apparent. Answers started to flow to me during nights, in meditations, in the middle of a conversation with someone, and especially, when I was writing in my journal. Now, I could not have stopped my healing journey anymore.

I came to realize that the key to my questions lay in understanding the belief systems of my family. The family patterns - as I accustomed to call them - are the subconscious conditioning of our minds that we received from our family and society. Most people would agree that parents affect their children. But what I learned is that it goes way beyond that. It is not only about the obvious, but it is mostly about the concealed. For rewriting my story and going beyond where my ancestors did, I needed to travel to the darkness. I had to be willing to look at what others did not want to see. At that, which stays in the shadow of our awareness.

The family patterns do not end with what our parents have taught us. Also, our parents' emotions, thoughts, and energy influence us. As quantum physics shows, everything is energy. Nothing is as solid as it seems. The same applies to emotions and thoughts. Although we cannot touch them or see them, thoughts leave our system in the form of energy waves whenever we think or feel. Then these invisible frequencies flow into our environment and continue living their own life from that moment on. Thus, I was conscious of the fact that the unspoken played a significant role in understanding my past too.

My body, just like yours, can capture the energy thought forms that fill up the ether around us. Besides, our bodies also interpret the energy of other people's thoughts and feelings. We just do not know about it because this inherent process is so flawless that we can transcribe the energies of others as our own. When you meet someone uplifting, their joy contaminates you. You cannot but be happy with them. Even though you may have felt bad just a while ago.

The bodily process that transcribes energies from our environment is instant. We feel other people's feelings as our own, and that is why we do even not realize that we do it. It is seamless magic. We swim in an endless ocean of energies, and thus we are interconnected with everything as if we were one living organism.

By observing my environment, I already knew that our parents create basic energy blueprints that form our behavior. Even before we were born, our little bodies downloaded information from our parents. Energetically we knew their emotions and thoughts while we were still in the womb. We got accustomed to those energies, and they slowly sank into our bodies. After we were born, our center of awareness was not developed yet. On the contrary, we perceived the world emotionally, and we allowed our subconscious mind to interpret the world around us.

The subconscious mind collects information, such as what kind of mood mom has or about the relationship of our parents, and then it saves it to the place where we forget about it. We only remember a tiny fraction of what we have ever learned, experienced, said, heard, or felt. Yet, all the intelligence is recorded in our minds the same way you would save data on the external disc of your computer. You can access the data at any moment, but you need to know how to use the external disc. Until we are about seven years old, the critical thinking that discerns whether the information is correct is not yet fully developed.

Thus when we are children, we rarely judge what our parents unconsciously teach us. Instead, we take it as written law, and later it serves as our blueprint for coping with life. Since this process is unconscious, we do not realize which past experiences impact our present choices. If your mom felt depressed, your body grew accustomed to the energy of depression, and you develop a tendency to feel low spirits too. The energy is already within you if you have not neutralized it. Once something activates it, the subconscious mind starts to play the old movie of seeing your mom feeling bad. Except for this time, you think that it is you who feels bad because you feel it in your own body, and you believe that the movie is happening to you.

Being armored with this knowledge, I knew precisely why my life looked the way it did. One part of me wished to change it while the other part was scared because even though I was unhappy, this way of life felt familiar. But my excitement about a new potential future eventually outgrew my fear of the unknown. I needed to change.

What I had unconsciously learned in my childhood ran the show of my previous life. It had always been that way, yet now, I was conscious of it and could write a new script for my future. I knew that if I could fully unlock my subconscious mind, I would transform my life. The gap between where I was and where I wanted to be would get smaller. However, now came the challenging task – to review my past and see how it made me the person I had become. And, more importantly, to see how I could bridge the gap and grow beyond my past. I did not want my past to define me anymore; I wished to use it as a fuel to change the direction of my life.

CHAPTER 3

BRONA

Your Spirit was saddened,
Your eyes were covered.
Nothing could have brightened
The distant places you traveled.

Only a peal of distant laughter
Reaches your ears.
It could never have been a happy bearer
During all those long eighty years.

Until the last days,
A little girl was locked in your heart,
Hidden from your sight in an opaque haze,
Redeeming her would be a piece of art.

Still, you became my family,
Brought me the painful destiny,
The one that was passed onto you,
Even though it was never true.

The night I entered this world was covered with a good dose of mystery. My mom would repeat the story to me whenever I asked, and I would often ask until I remembered it by heart. Something would draw me to the story of my birth as if there was information that I would later be able to understand.

In the afternoon of the day that I was born, my mom still painted the corridor walls of our house. A couple of hours later, she started to feel contractions, and my father drove her to a hospital. That night my mom was alone in a big regional hospital. The nurses had left, the doctor was sleeping, and no other babies were born during that night. The maternity ward seemed utterly empty.

Before the doctor left, he assured my mom that she was going to give birth the following morning, and he advised her to get some sleep. After a couple of hours, a beautiful summer day turned into a windy night. All of a sudden, the wind blast opened the windows of my mom's room, and a storm began. At that exact moment, my mom went into labor all by herself. I was born within fifteen minutes, shortly before midnight. According to my mom, the storm stopped as quickly as it had started after I took my first breaths. The next morning, the hospital returned to its normal mode and was soon filled with other mothers and their babies. For the first two weeks, my skin and hair color was a complete opposite to what it is now to the point that my parents doubted whether someone exchanged me by accident. However, since only mom gave birth during that summer night, it was unlikely. After two weeks, my hair turned blond, and my skin lightened up.

I spent my childhood in an old house in the Border Mountains of Bohemia. My maternal grandma, Brona, raised me until I went to school. Brona was Polish, and destiny brought her to Czechoslovakia after the Second World War. I recall Brona being a practical woman; she showed her love in ways that were challenging for others to recognize. However, after deciphering her patterns, it became simpler to grasp Brona's complex personality. She had been shaped into a strict woman by her difficult childhood.

Brona was about nine years old when she was taken away from her family in Poland and sent into forced labor in Nazi Germany. In fact, this turned out to be a better destiny for her.

At first, Brona was sent by train to the concentration camp in Auschwitz. It would usually mean a one-way ticket. For reasons still unknown to me, the Nazi soldiers took little Brona away from her large family of farmers, who had a couple of houses in a small Polish village. I never understood why they took only my grandmother and allowed other siblings and parents to stay together. Sometimes destiny works in mysterious ways. I can only imagine how hard it must have been for her because she would never reveal her feelings to anyone. I do not dare to say how long it took for her to process what had happened or whether she ever found peace within her. The first time, Brona shared her story with me was when I was eight years old because I insisted. I would always have many questions for everyone and would never stop before I got the answers.

So it happened that little Brona found herself alone on the train to the concentration camp. She never said whether she realized where she was going. But I believe that she did not know, and it was perhaps better that way. When they arrived in Auschwitz, Brona stepped out of the train, with dozens of other Polish people disappearing through the main gate of the camp.

When she reached the gate, suddenly, a Nazi soldier put his hand in front of her to indicate that she was not going into the camp. Perhaps it was her blue eyes and blonde hair that saved her life, or maybe the mercy of the soldier. Either way, she was saved. The soldier gave an order to send Brona to Germany to work for a family farm. She stayed there for the entirety of the war. Every day, Brona had to get up before the sunrise to do the chores on the farm. Together with other young people who perhaps had experienced something similar, she took care of the cattle, the household, and the agricultural fields. My mom once told me that although the work was hard and monotonous, the wife of the wealthy man who owned the farm was kind to Brona. Mom thinks that the lady felt sorry for my grandmother and perhaps cherished some maternal instincts for her.

After the Second World War, Brona traveled to Prague, the capital city of the Czech Republic. I learned from Brona's narration that many people would find new homes in Prague after the war. Perhaps people hoped that Czechoslovakia would recapture the success of the pre-war years. Between the World Wars, Czechoslovakia belonged to the top ten of the most developed countries in the world.

Brona found a job in a hotel in the center of Prague, where she stayed for about a year and a half. She did not wish to return to Poland, at least not for some time. Then the fate intervened once again. One day, Brona received an invitation from a friend who lived in the north of the country. When Brona's visit was nearing the end, they went dancing, and that night Brona met her future husband, my grandfather, Jerome.

Jerome was a tall, good-looking man, and Brona and Jerome connected instantly. His sense of freedom and human rights had always been palpable. Although he did not have to do it, he volunteered to join the Czech army in Paris at the beginning of the war. Since Czechoslovakia was surrendered to Germany in 1938, there was no war in my homeland. We had a Nazi Protectors who governed our country, and mostly German families lived in our border areas. Thus Jerome would not have to fight in the war, but he was always a warrior in his heart for the things that mattered.

Shortly he became fluent in French and English, and after some time, he was transferred to London, where he became an RAF pilot. When he was fighting, he never worried about his life. Although Jerome had a family with three little children in London, he was fearless. After the war, he left the UK, and Jerome and his wife split. His ex-wife did not want to take care of their three children, and to my knowledge, she never attempted to find them or contact them again. Life would lead Jerome to return to Czechoslovakia as a single father of three children. So, after he met my grandmother, Brona became the mother of three.

After the war, Jerome received many honors, both from the UK and Czechoslovakia. As one of the rewards for his services during the Second World War, he received a house with a large garden on returning home. However, the happiness and relief after the war did not last long, and soon events took an abrupt turn. Only three years after the war, he was not a hero anymore. He became a threat to the communists who took over the country in 1948 and held it under their sway for the following forty-one years.

The highest-ranking communists had no other personal aspirations but to climb up the party ladder. No wonder they felt threatened by independent and capable people because it was difficult to control them. That was why they needed to use any and all forms of persecution. Jerome was first signed to work at an airport for small aircrafts, but later, he was transferred to work as a gas station attendant – where he would be perfectly harmless. This was painful for Jerome as he was a strong and vigorous man with an independent spirit. He wanted to be a creator of his own destiny, but it was not possible under the communist regime. I suppose he never found peace with that political system.

After Jerome and Brona moved together, she had to take care of the children, the house, and a vast garden where they had some cattle and grew vegetables. Brona also became a cook, and I can imagine how many responsibilities she must have had in her early twenties if not in late teens. I do not know how old Brona was after the war because she lied about her age. She made herself older, probably by four years, and I never knew her real age.

Before my mom was born, Brona and Jerome had a son, who unfortunately died at the age of sixteen on borreliosis. At the early stages of the disease, the doctors said that he feigned his headaches because he did not want to go to school. Later, when they finally found out about his condition, it was too late. He was dying slowly in great pains for a decade.

I believe that this was probably part of the reason why Brona hung too much on my mom – both in a good and a wicked sense. I believe that Brona grew hard because she was traumatized by a series of painful moments of her life. In order to cope with her life and the communist regime, which was challenging for my whole family, she separated herself from her feelings as many people would do after the war. Amid hardships, it may seem more natural to numb the feelings.

Otherwise, one could get easily overwhelmed by the circumstances, and there was still a family to show up for every day. However, this seemingly straightforward choice did not make Brona and anyone else happy. As in many other post-war marriages, my grandparents became rather practical and wanted to keep the family going. On top of that, one never knew if and when they could attain their freedom again, Brona and Jerome focused on the tasks at hand. They had no place in their hearts for any great dreams or hopes of a better future. Since the cruel reality, under the communistic regime, did not allow for prospects of better days ahead. Brona dealt with it better than Jerome, who believed in equality and in the right of people to determine their own lives.

Another disaster came along when Jerome suffered from lung cancer for many years. My mom remembers how one day she came home from school and found her father in tears of desperations while holding a gun in his hands, wondering whether he should take his own life. Although he decided to continue fighting cancer, he eventually died when my mom was seventeen.

All these undeniable moments formed Brona's character to appear tough to other people. Hence, she displayed love to my mom by being pedant and strict. Possibly Brona wanted to protect my mom from falling in love with someone all too early. Thus she would not allow her much freedom. Brona's hardworking demeanor also led my mom to manual work in the house and the garden, and in some ways, that was the sign of Brona's love. Everyone has their own love language. Yours can be words when another shows you their admiration through loving assurances. Brona's love language was manual labor, and she believed that this was the best way to raise my mom.

Although my mom employed the same love language, later on, I believe that she secretly wanted Brona to nurture her as her baby girl. She would prefer Brona to buy her a lovely dress or hug her when she felt sad. A loving word would have been more supportive of my mom's young spirit than the strict regime.

These memories have provoked many questions in me.

No wonder I had many family patterns. Just like Brona's experience shaped her personality, she, in turn, did forge the character of my mom. Since Brona could not express her love to my mom, my mom also struggled to do the same. And as a result of it, I grew to believe that no one could love me and also that it hurt to love someone else. Later on, my subconscious mind would always make me run away from love. It reminded me of the pain that I had felt when I was young and how it tried to prevent me from any potential pain in my romantic relationships.

It is both a breathtaking and scary idea that we come into this world already predetermined by our ancestors. What if I would be different without those patterns? What was my real self untouched by the inner demons passed down by generations? And, most of all, where does free will begin?

CHAPTER 4

THE CHILDHOOD MEMORIES

The sacred mission of each relationship
Is to grow us into our potential.
Often disguised as a hardship,
We struggle to remain masterful.

The dearest of people push our buttons,
As we misinterpret their teaching.
We unleash the enraged dragons
And let our hearts be forever aching.

Let me taste my divine lesson.
May my hearing be blessed with patience,
Or else, I stay imprisoned in immortal tension,
And never savor my soul's radiance.

Let the past deeds now be forgiven.
I spent too many years replaying them in my head.
From now on, may my life be brightened!
May love become my daily bread.

As an empath, I can also experience my life experiences based on my feelings, intuition, visions, and knowing. I can recall how each situation made me feel as if it happened just now, and I can also remember the smell in the air, what others felt at that moment, or the way they looked at me. Being an empath has allowed me to go beyond the what and when; it has allowed me to see how and why. The reason why something happened would always become apparent when I regained my balance. That is why it never truly mattered what people told me because I could read their intentions and energy through my own body. Others could not lie to me because often I knew things that they could not even admit to themselves. I could see beyond the surface.

As I was thinking about my childhood, a memory surfaced in my mind. It is the first memory I have from this life. Still, I could see it clearly as a movie playing in my mind's eyes. I must have been less than one year old as I was still sleeping in a crib. One day, as I was lying there, I saw various 3D shapes in the air in front of me. I reached out to touch them, and my hand went through.

These energies were forming distinct geometrical patterns, and somehow I comprehended their meaning. I cannot explain how I understood the message or why I still remember those shapes, but this is something I could always do. The energy communicated with me and revealed some crucial moments of my future. I understood that my life was going to be challenging at first, but I also intuitively knew that I was protected and that someone non-physical would always look after me. I think that it was my first conscious contact, both with my soul and my spirit guides. My soul revealed my future to me at the energy level, so I would never forget it.

Although recalling my first memory filed me with love and hope, what followed it did not. Every time I would think about my childhood, a wave of sadness spread through my body. This time it was no different. I have perceived the energy of my childhood as a dark cloud hovering above the house we lived in. Energy never disappears by itself. Therefore to lighten it up, it must be transformed into another form of frequency. Everything that had happened in our old house and the development of events during and after the war was like a dark cloud spreading over my whole hometown. Moreover, the sorrowful lives of Brona, Jerome, and of my aunts and uncles still hung onto us energetically for a long time.

The first six years of my life were inseparably linked to Brona. She was my everything. We all lived in the same house, but there were three separate flats. I lived on the first floor with her until I was six, while my brother and parents lived on the second and third floors. Although my parents did their best for my brother and me, they never explained to me why I lived with my grandmother. During the first six years of my life, I can remember seeing my parents only occasionally. We made a few trips together on the weekends, celebrated birthdays and Christmases, and I would sometimes play with my brother in their flat. Besides that, I had quite a lot of freedom.

Brona was always in motion. She often did some housework, or she would take care of our garden. Thus, I had enough space, sometimes even too much space, to be on my own. When I was at home, I would play alone only with the use of my imagination, which was one of the greatest gifts. When I was outside, I could run freely in our garden or the far-reaching meadow in front of our house. Although I enjoyed both, I would still often feel lonely. I believed that there was something wrong with me because I did not share the same flat with my parents. The feelings of separation and rejection deeply seeded in me. I felt invisible to others.

It was challenging for a little child to comprehend that others perhaps have problems unrelated to her. I struggled to feel loved because others did not pay much attention to me, and I did not have an opportunity to develop a strong bond with my parents, who were mostly absent during the first six years of my life. Love used to be a missing element in my life. Only later, as an adult, I genuinely understood what love meant. It was back then in that old house when I started to crave for love and appreciation. Each day, I would wake up and hope that everything would be fine, and I would be with my whole family, but that dream did not seem to come true.

Without understanding it back then, I cried for attention by developing a strong nosebleed. I often used to suffer from it. I would wake up in the middle of the night to find my pillow and blanket covered with blood. My mom came to clean it sometimes. Other times Brona did it. Now I know how the mind-body connection works, so I realize that I unconsciously created this experience to obtain my mom's attention.

Naturally, the nosebleed did not help strengthen the connection between my mom and me. Our bond has always been complicated, and it started with Brona. Although you could always count on Brona, she was emotionally unavailable. Above that, I remember how she often argued with others using unkind words. For my own good, it was better not to catch too much of her attention. Once when I was brushing my hair, the comb got stuck in my long locks. I was about three years old and asked Brona to help me. Without any discussion or warning, she took scissors and cut off my long hair. This was Brona, direct, without any sugar-coating, always focused on doing.

Brona raised my mom in the same manner, and that may be the reason why I never felt my mom's love. And still, I believe that she never meant anything wrong, she just did not find the key to her own happiness. There was a void in my chest that nothing could fill in. The one thing that I wanted the most, I could not receive. In time, I learned to live with that feeling, but it had not started to heal until 2012. I thought that I must have done something wrong that I did not receive my mom's love. Over and over, the feelings of guilt made me doubt myself. "What did I do wrong? Why does no one care about me? Does it even matter that I exist?" These thoughts were playing on a loop in my head.

Although I never stopped hoping for things to improve, I stopped believing they would. The dark cloud hovering above our house infiltrated the hearts and minds of all of us and made us feel separated from each other. I know that I was not the only one who felt sadness, my mom felt it, too. But my every attempt to reach out to her failed, they pushed her even further away from me. I knew that she had her share of unresolved emotions and challenges, but I hoped that perhaps I could make her happy. If she was unhappy, I failed.

As I was growing up, I noticed that the best approach to escape anger was to stay quiet and invisible. When I was closed in a Brona's bedroom where I also slept, I did not bother anyone, no one would get upset or sad. I trained myself to suppress my vital energy and excitement about nature and God, and I became silent until someone would ask me something. However, no one would ask me much anything. This seeded a belief in me that it was better to be obedient and submissive, although it went against my natural self. Day by day, I grew into a conclusion that I needed to hold my rich inner world under the lock where no one could see it. I would avoid any potentially conflicting situations, and I would carefully choose diplomatic words that would make everyone happy, although they did not express my genuine thoughts.

When I was six, right before I went to school, we all moved into a new house together. And so, a new chapter of my life opened for me. I was excited to go to school, which I enjoyed since the first day, and on top of that, I finally got my own tiny room. In my heart, I also believed that things would get better in our family, and they did a little. However, as we lived under one roof, I began to notice another aspect that I had been blissfully unaware of.

This was the first time that my brother and I shared a common space. Over the years, I could see that my parents gave him love and support. I also noticed that he was misusing this privilege, which made me often feel irritated because although I did my best to do everything the right way, mom would often be upset with me for no apparent reason. This sent me even further into self-doubt and insecurity.

From my current understanding, I could pinpoint the moment when I stopped fighting for my dreams. I believed that I would fail to reach them anyway because I lacked my parent's support, or if I succeeded, my parents would not register it anyway. The subconscious equation in my mind ran, "No matter what I do, mom is upset with me and sends me negative energy that I do not know how to cope with. It seems that it bothers her that I am in "her" house," as she made it clear on many occasions. Little by little, I would give up everything before I even truly tried.

On the other hand, living together also brought brighter aspects. Occasionally I would have philosophical conversations with my dad. My dad has always been kind to us children. Although he would spend a considerable part of his free time with my brother, we would also sometimes discuss topics that were close to my heart. I can recall the evenings when we discussed exciting topics ranging from ancient history to God. My dad was like a walking encyclopedia because he remembered many facts. Although he would often confuse the names, I still learned a lot from him in my early teenage years. I loved talking about ghosts, the soul, the universe, the aliens, the purpose of life, the physics, and so on.

He also helped me deal better with some nonphysical encounters. He would always remind me that Jesus showed us the only path. But I was never a Christian, nor was my family in the traditional sense. I mostly relied on my own experiences and on my own heart. I never studied religions, so I am not that familiar with their teachings, but people would often tell me that I speak like a Buddhist or Taoist. Still, I have always felt close to the teachings of Jesus Christ because I could feel them in my heart without studying them.

However, at some point, when I was around eighteen years old, I started to have some deeper experiences that I could not share as freely as I used to with my dad. Gradually without me noticing it at first, I started to feel that some of my spiritual experiences were too much for him. Not that he would be unable to comprehend them, but it was more about the fear which my experiences and findings triggered in him. It is common to fear that which we cannot explain. So I knew that I was on my own from that point on.

CHAPTER 5

THE UNTOLD TRUTH

My life was like a silver leaf,
Sharply pointed towards the edges,
Filled with mystery and grief.
Sometimes my body was pulled by sleds,
Dragging me to the demon's net.

All the people, all the voices
Are mere figures guiding me to return.
The free will and power of my choices
Led me to an unexpected turn
For my lips to taste the sovereignty of my soul.

When the dark night set in,
I could witness my glow.
When the morning came in,
The magic disappeared, and I felt low,
Feeling every person's essence in my heart.

During the days, I felt their pain,
I observed their struggles
Holding tight like an infinite chain.
They would come as hundreds
To prevent me from finding a quiet space.

My name, Sylvia, originates from the Latin word Silva, which means the spirit of the wood, the one from the forests, or a forest fairy. The names hold power and can reveal much about a person. I believe that names carry the essence of a person. In my case, Sylvia is the perfect name to describe my connection with the forest. Forest is my kingdom, the place where the world makes sense, and where I feel protected and grounded.

For every sensitive soul, time alone is not a luxury; it is a matter of survival. The fact that I could always feel other people's feelings within myself made me seek solitude every now and then. Sometimes I needed to disappear daily into the forest. There, undisturbed and surrounded by animals and trees, I could catch a breath and reconnect with the life itself.

When I still lived with my family, I would often go for a walk in the forest with our dogs. In the quietness, utterly hidden from others, I could regain balance and process my emotions. The forest always embraced me with calmness and love. I was connecting there with the universe and my heart. And even when my heart was filled with pain, it all seemed to dissipate when I lay in the grass.

One day, I took our Dogue de Bordeaux, Bono, and headed to the forest. I avoided the beaten tracks and walked to my favorite spot up on a hill. As I arrived in my favorite place, I sat down on a fine moss. All I could hear was the chirping of birds and the heavy breathing of my dog, who would always want to go for a run and change his mind only after a couple of meters.

That day, it was one of those ordinary days when I felt weary of how unequally my parents treated my brother and me. Sometimes, I felt like bubbling inside when I listened to his conversations with my parents. They almost worshiped him. Had I been equally troublesome as he, my mom would punish me with complete ignorance and withdrawal for days while talking ugly about me to others as she often did. However, I never witnessed her doing the same to my brother. It seemed to me that he could not fail in her eyes, and no matter what I did, it never was enough. I put my head on my knees and began to cry. Once again, I asked God why I needed to experience a lack of love. What was the purpose of my life when no one seemed to love me or even care for me?

Like any child, I wanted my family to love and support me. I did not feel like I belonged. Not only in my family but nowhere really. I did my best to fit in and talk about clothes and boys with my girlfriends to make them think that I was one of them. I did it, although my mind was always preoccupied with different topics. It was not typical for little girls to think about history, the universe, or counting on three sheets of paper the size of our galaxy. It felt as if I was wired to only think about these topics. Honestly, nothing has changed much since I was a child, but I learned to share this part of me more openly.

Trying to fit in was hurting me and driving me crazy. Many conversations were too dull for me, but I stayed and smiled anyway to make others feel like I was interested. "What would happen if I were myself?" I wondered many times. "Well, I guess that I would be totally alone. Without friends. Destined to become a monk," my ego readily replied. My ego feared that I would be that weird girl who can help you find your life calling and talk about the secret history but does not know anything about handbags and shoes.

As I was sitting under a tree, I realized that day by day, I was losing connection with my soul. In the beginning, I had only wanted to hide a little piece of myself to gain acceptance from others. Gradually I had become the only person who knew my true self. Or did I?

In the safety of the forest, I recalled a recent interaction with my family that left me to feel utterly abandoned. I felt that a thick wall separated me from my family, and I had no clue of how to overcome it. They seemed to be one unit – the family. While I was on the sidelines, alone, and observing them. I could not shake off the feeling of being an alien element in their family. The only thing that gave me strength was the birth of my little sister. I prayed for having a sister for so long. And then, when I was ten and a half, my prayer was answered. I wanted her to have a beautiful childhood, so I started to take care of her, to play with her, and to teach her how to walk and talk. She got so used to me that eventually, she would not fall asleep without me putting her to bed.

Even though my sister was a gift to me, I was gravely wounded in my soul, and I could not see a way out. I never saw it coming, but gradually my pure and light essence metamorphosed into sorrow. Like a dark mist, it covered my thinking. The heavy pressure of all the unhealed family patterns changed me. I allowed it to happen because, back then, I did not understand the dynamics of family patterns. Subconsciously I hoped that by accepting their world, I would get closer to my family and stop feeling like an alien. My heart was whispering to me that there was nothing wrong with me, but my mind kept persuading that the unhappiness of my family was entirely my fault.

I also felt responsible for my parent's happiness. Foolishly I thought that I could fix everything if I met their expectations. Thus I learned to ignore the voice of my heart. I chose the wrong counselor. But at that time, I did not comprehend how our choices gradually shape us. I departed from my heart and dove into self-doubts, sadness, and despair. The only bright moments came about when I was alone. Like waving a magic wand, solitude always healed me in a matter of seconds.

Bono interrupted my train of thoughts as he insisted on leaving. He placed his muzzle into my lap and looked at me with his sad eyes asking, "Do we have to sit here so long? Everyday? Is it necessary?" "Well, yes, my dear dog," I said out loud. "I want to process my feelings and catch a new breath, and all you care about is to leave. I know that once we come home, you will be scrounging to go for a walk again. I know you too well." Then I cuddled with him for a moment.

Before returning home from my walk, I reflected on my desire to receive love from my parents. This yearning for love has the power to alter us to become a person we assume we need to be to deserve someone's feelings. "How free would I be had I not searched for my parent's love?" I knew that I had to find a way out of my personal hell.

Instinctively I understood that I could not afford to victimize myself for much longer, or my true self would flee for good. Then a sudden realization washed over me on my way back home. For an instant, the lightness entered my mind, and I saw everything with a regained touch of clarity. The reason why I was surrounded by unhappy people, and they could not treat me the way I wanted was to make me stronger. The reason was not that I was an unlovable person, the purpose of all this was to make me find love within myself.

It was not meant to break me, it was to help me connect with God, the universe, and with myself. In that flash of awareness, I saw myself helping others to reconnect with their true selves so that they could also step into their inner power. The infinite power that comes from the soul and is independent of anything and anyone else. Enthusiastically, I accepted the invitation to find myself, and I jotted it down in my diary as soon as I arrived home so that I would never forget this sudden stream of consciousness.

CHAPTER 6

TASTING MY LIGHT

I wish to find my light before it flees.
The moment we enjoy together is so brief!
Before the darkness takes over our minds,
And we forget that we are children of Light.

How many times have I yearned for you?
For you are my only home.
Nothing that comes from this world is true,
The illusions make us nothing but roam.

My soul, please, fill me up with your Light!
Let me embody your essence
And help me touch the stars.
Let me feel God's substance.

How many lifetimes have I traveled to this old, newfound
place,
That now shelters my human body and earths my soul?
Still, I am not of this world; my essence is of stardust lace,
My heart needs the Breath of Life to make it pound.

I entered the galaxies, I traveled the space,
My inner light forever guides me on my way.
From our chest reaches out a Golden ray
To lead us back from the darkest place.

When I find you,

I do not need others.
I can discern what is true,
And I take off my blinders.

You have always been there,
Yet I had not seen you.
Now my mind is filled with glare,
And everything seems freshly new.

If I could hold onto you,
I know that all the wounds could be healed.
But I know the dark times will return out of the blue.
No matter which land I go, there is no shield.

I am not sure whether everyone is conscious of it, but at some point in our life, a split happens. We lose our childlike innocence and become as our society expects us to be. Gradually we buy into the beliefs of our friends, family, and culture and accept their reality as ours.

Before the split happened, we knew that everything would ultimately turn out well. Our hearts pulsated with life and enthusiasm, and most importantly, we were filled with unshakable faith. Our innocence was rooted in our belief that the world is a kind and safe place. Then something shook our world, and we stopped feeling secure. Somewhere along the way, we began to believe in the world that is dangerous and hostile. This one seed of doubt spread into a stubborn weed that now overshadows our thinking. When we begin to perceive the world as a hostile place, we need to separate ourselves from others to protect our lives and identities. However, we cannot feel separate from others unless we detach from ourselves first.

So, the inner split transpires. Along with our innocent self, a doubtful, dark self is born. While growing up, I was aware of the split, years before it came. Slowly I was losing myself in exchange for acceptance. At first, it was a conscious choice, a calculated path of the least resistance. It was easier to hide some parts of me not to make others upset. To some extent, it was a game for me. I knew what others wanted me to do and what they needed to hear to leave me in peace and in my inner world where I felt home.

Although the feeling of sadness was real, the choice to alter me to fit in was a conscious choice. It was my response to the pain that I carried within. I would do my best to avoid having controversial conversations, although it did not always work out. Already when I was little, I noticed that specific topics that were out of the traditional scope would trigger a vast range of emotions in people. Others would do anything to protect their truth even though it was built on assumptions, not knowledge.

Still, until I turned fourteen, I was in touch with my innocent self. The mask that I wore in front of certain people did not own me yet; I was in control of it. In my inner world, I knew who I was. There was not a second that I would not feel the Source. Closed behind the doors of my tiny room, I would ponder about the galaxies and feel into the star-spangled universe. I could feel the universe flowing in every cell of my body. To me, there were no boundaries, no separation among the creations of God. It felt as if my body became liquid, and I merged with the essence of life. The gift of feeling God has always been the one thing that would bring me back, no matter how far into the underworld I traveled. Regardless of how imperfect my outside reality may have been, it never threatened my connection with

God. On the contrary, it strengthened it.

I remember that at some point, I cried myself into sleep every night. I felt the chasm between my family and myself, and there would not be a day when I did not wish to be an adult already, so I could finally leave home. Little did I know that you carry your home with you wherever you go until you heal your past and choose your own path. But even in those moments, I did not feel abandoned by God. My connection with the universe and God would eventually always soothe me. It was my true origin.

When I turned ten, my true self won me over entirely for over three years. The trigger moment that helped me to remember my true self came unexpectedly during a Czech language class at school. During the writing exercise, the teacher asked us to spell out the word "pyramid." I may have misspelled it, but the word kept resounding in my head until the school finished. As I walked home, I could not stop thinking about that magical word, although I had no idea what it meant. I felt like I knew the word "pyramid," but it was all blurred like a dream. I could almost remember what it meant, but not quite yet. It opened up something unknown within me.

As soon as I arrived home, I hurried to the kitchen where my mom was baking, and I asked her what a pyramid was. She explained it to me, but it did not satisfy my curiosity. So, I went into my brother's room because I remembered that he had got a book about ancient Rome, Greece, and Egypt the previous Christmas. When I found the book, I began reading about ancient Egypt. I read it whole in one breath, but it invoked in me more questions than it offered answers, and I became even more eager to learn more.

A month later, during the summer holiday, I went to the city library with my best friend, and we both got our first library card. Now I finally had time to study something interesting as opposed to the shallow stuff at school. The librarian looked up at me sheepishly when I lay my twenty books on her counter, and she pointed out that the monthly limit was ten books. Unwillingly, I selected only ten books and hurried home where my love affair with Egypt soon blossomed.

Each day, I would spend hours flipping through the pages of those books. Next to me, I had a 200-page notebook that mom had given me, and I used it to take notes. On the first page of my journal, I wrote down the Egyptian alphabet with hieroglyphs, followed by all the names of the kings and pharaohs who are officially known. On each page, I would also inscribe my name into the cartouche as the Egyptians used to do. When I got my first radio player later, I would also record my notes and thoughts about what I was reading on cassettes as well as write them down.

After the new school year started, my fascination with Egypt continued and grew even stronger. I hurried from school and did my homework immediately without taking a break so I would have enough time for my Egyptian studies. Although I would not consider myself a disciplined person, I gladly followed the self-imposed routine.

Later on, I discovered the theories and books of Erich von Däniken, who advocates an alternative explanation of human history. He and many other ancient archeologists believe that our human evolution was influenced by extraterrestrials. As shocking as it may sound to most people, it never sounded alien to me. Having an infinite universe for only one race on one planet would be a mere waste of space, and it would also imply that we are the master race of the universe, which with all the respect I never believed. Däniken and others support their theories with proofs that are difficult to argue with. However, only a few selected people choose what the mainstream archeology claims to be true. If different people were to write the history books, we would believe in something else. After all, no one remembers those ancient times unless we tap into our Akashic memories. Thus we are dependent on how some authorities interpret the clues left behind. And people have their own unconscious agendas coupled to their truths.

Around that time, my most favorite TV-series, Stargate, started. I would watch it every day, and we would discuss it with my dad, who loved it as much as I did. While watching the journeys of the SG team traveling to other planets through a stargate found in Giza, a new passion sparked in me – the universe. After learning and understanding the fundamental theories about the universe, I figured that quantum physics was the nearest to describe some of the phenomena that I had experienced through my heightened states of consciousness. Although I could still see some shortcomings in quantum physics, finally, I had something that partially described my perception of reality.

My enchantment with the universe and Egypt was tangible. During those three years, I controlled myself much less and let my enthusiasm be seen. I would have hours of monologues to explain Egypt to others. Eventually, my mom promised to take me to Egypt when I would turn eighteen. However, I could not stop talking about it, so we visited Egypt already when I was thirteen. It was such an achievement! I must have been truly annoying talking about Egypt all the time!

First, we flew to Cairo, and even though it was nighttime, I could see the three giant shapes rising proudly in the darkness. In their magnitude, the rest of the city felt uninteresting. My heart pounded fast because now I could see the pyramids with my own eyes. Egypt welcomed me with open arms, and I experienced many unplanned adventures. I was already familiar with every temple which we visited on our trip because of the books I had read. Thus I did not like to walk with the group and listen to the guide. In reality, people would come to me for more details about Egypt or learn what was written on a papyrus that they were planning to buy.

On our second day, after visiting the Great Pyramids of Giza, my mom and I were waiting for the rest of the group. Unexpectedly, a man came to me and suggested that I follow him. As naïve as it could seem, I did follow him. He led my mom and me to the three smaller, satellite pyramids on the right side of the Great Pyramids. Whoever that man was, he allowed us to go inside those pyramids and wanted nothing in return. No wonder, I was over the moon excited about it and spent a considerable amount of time inside those satellite pyramids.

The same luck accompanied us at every site we visited. From Giza, we traveled all the way south to Aswan, where we boarded on a Nile cruise ship that became our home for the next two weeks. We set off along the Nile toward the north and stopped at the most famous temples. There was a souvenir shop on the ship selling Egyptian statues and jewelry. The shopkeeper gifted me with a silver pedant symbolizing the Horus eye. When we came back to our cabin, I opened the bag and also spotted some other shiny objects. Although my mom and I never took our eyes off the shopkeeper, he must have put those other ancient Egyptian amulets to the bag. To this day, I do not know how the jewelry got into that bag and why he did not tell us about the surprise since he had already given me a gift. But I accepted it with a loving heart.

Those three years were happy because I embraced my uniqueness. I could be my true self alone in my room and sometimes with my parents and my best friend. Later I would often find strength in those memories. Unconsciously, I built up a foundation that has carried me ever since. During those years, my soul was near.

CHAPTER 7

SHADOWS

In your words, I hear isolated whispers,
Come closer to me, so I can hear.
Still, all I catch is a distant whir.
Your presence fills my chest with sorrow,
Instead of my heart, now there is a hole.

The mornings creep stealthily in.
The evenings have already gone.
Hold my hand and show me the way out
Into the world of hope,
Into the land of tomorrow.

As a black mage, you left my body on a cold floor,
Lying there naked begging for help.
Long ago, I forgot my own halo.
When you are closer, you transport me to a parallel realm,
The warmth of your body reaches my cells.

Please, help me to remember who I used to be.
Remind me of my light and beauty.
My spirit is rising and dares to be free.
Although my sight can only see the shadows now,
My heart senses a way to my true home.

Egypt changed me. As we traveled from one ancient temple
to another, we embarked on a journey similar to the one that

Egyptian priests and priestess used to take to be initiated into the sacred teachings and mysteries. Unconsciously, I came to Egypt for the same reason. My steps led me to Egypt to experience the sacred initiation, which was only the first of many initiations that followed. However, that time, it was not an initiation into my inner light, but into my darkness. Until that point, I did not comprehend the darkness except as my feelings of deep sadness. After Egypt, I slowly began connecting with the dark side within me, which led to less than happy nine years of my life.

My dad once said to me, "Everyone has both light and darkness within them. One cannot live without both. If you tried to get rid of your dark side completely, it would be as if you opened the front door for any thief. Then it would be easy for someone to come along and take over your house. The dark side, or the evil, protects you from an even greater evil." Despite I was about nine years old when he first told me, I immediately understood what he meant. My dad would often use simple analogies to explain some more profound concepts. I knew that we should not aim to suppress the dark side within us, but instead, we should learn to use it for our growth and transmute it to light. And so, my training with the darkness began after Egypt.

At first, the transition into my shadow was not noticeable. On the surface, my life continued flowing ordinarily, but my thoughts and emotions were metamorphosing. The little protective bubble that enabled me to cope with my family and the world suffered some severe cracks. Over time, I stopped trying to prove myself to my parents, and I resigned from my efforts to make them treat my brother and me equally. Although this would be a smart decision, I chose to stop caring out of victimhood rather than acceptance.

When Brona still lived, I spent a considerable amount of time with her. Although I dare to say that I was her favorite in our family, our conversations were not always pleasant. I hope that she was unconscious of it, but she had the habit of putting people down, myself included. Over the years, I got used to her manner of speaking. On the other hand, I appreciated her for always listening to what I wanted to share. At that point, she was not so active as she used to be, so I would come to her room, and we would sit on a balcony and talk. Brona was not satisfied with how things unfolded between my parents, which made us two with the same opinion. In our home, the surge of unhappiness was always hanging in the air.

By the time when I turned thirteen, I was already studying at a bilingual grammar school, which also meant new friends and habits for me. Each of my classmates had a distinct personality, and thus my weirdness was not as striking as in elementary school. On the other hand, no one was into spirituality, philosophy, or Egypt. Instead, my ex-classmates loved to gossip about people and their clothes. For me, those conversations were challenging because I did not care about any of it. Only because I wanted to have at least some friends in that school, I would try to have a funny comment or pretend that I agreed.

During the first two years in grammar school, we were all getting to know each other, and our class was rather intimate. Then new classmates joined, and the new dynamics divided our class into small groups. One day before the summer holiday, I learned that the guys in our class did not like a girl who was sort of a friend of mine. As soon as I learned about it, I felt sorry for her and wanted to save her. That day something tipped the scales, and I knew that I needed to choose to which group I belonged. I chose to become a close friend of that girl. Thus I did what I often did in my friendships; I tried to save someone.

It was a crucial decision because our friendship let me encounter my shadow. Soon we became inseparable, and we would talk for hours after school and call each other during the weekends as she lived in another city. In the summer before my sixteenth birthday, she asked me to accompany her to a rock party. I used to listen to pop and other optimistic music, but she loved rock and metal music, and after that party, I slowly converted to rock too. Eventually, my whole wardrobe turned black.

It was the first party for me, and my parents allowed me to stay until midnight. As the devil would have it, as my dad says, we met there a group of guys who became the center points of our universes for the next two years. The guys were funny and charming, and we connected instantly. My friend and I developed a crush on two of the most mysterious of those guys. Obviously, for a teenage girl, the stranger guy, the better. Or was it just me? I was never interested in the mainstream guys who tried too much to look good. Guys who visited the gym and carefully worked the gel into their hair bored me. Although those well-put-together guys liked me and would often invite me for a date, I refused them. Instead, I preferred the long-haired weirdos who were unpopular, and they seemed to know something that no one else did.

Our new friends told us that they came to these parties twice a month and so we eventually started doing the same to spend yet another evening with them. I fell in love with Jacob, who was two years my senior and usually had a hood over his head and listened to Korn, which I adored by then.

I would spend more time with him at the rock parties, and a couple of months later, we would party every weekend. I would dance with Jacob until the early morning hours, and I was in love with everything he did or said. However, there was one disappointing aspect that I should have paid much more attention to.

Jacob's words did not meet his behavior, and he would shower me with empty promises. Having no experience in relationships, I would find an excuse after another for his behavior, but the truth was that he was breaking my heart. During that time, my sense of self-worth dropped to zero. Jacob was inconsistent in everything that he did, and I only found out later that he was playing the same tricks on other girls. I was not alone, and all of us girls were in love with him while he was perhaps just having fun. Little did I know that he was also a drug addict. My friends told me about his addiction about a decade later, and finally, his behavior made sense.

However, I would have appreciated learning about his addiction sooner before I foolishly allowed him to form my perception of romantic love. My self-esteem went up and down depending on his moods, and I started an unhealthy habit of pleasing men to receive their love in return. Little did I know how crucial those teenage years are for developing our confidence and our healthy sense of self. I became blind to his mistakes and shortcomings and would never allow myself to think something bad about him. Even though our relationship was painful, it was a necessary experience that allowed me to see the shadow aspects of myself.

I spent time with Jacob and his friends also because I did not want to be at home. When I was at home, all I could hear were daily arguments echoing from wall to wall. From early mornings till late evenings, the constant stress and unhappiness were tangible. I could not hide from it. The moment I entered our house, the dark cloud of energy rushed over me. Heaviness tightened my chest, and I wanted to either scream or cry, but could do neither.

The constant struggle for love and finances had always been the primary source of pressure in our home. My parents are entrepreneurs, and there seemed to be a continuous stream of unexpected problems that impacted our family climate. Since the office was in our dining hall, it was impossible for anyone to distance themselves from the business. I still remember the late-night calls from their employees who encountered some difficulties, which always got my parents into a panic. I needed stability and safe space, but instead of it, everything was changing every second and even the moods of my parents. Since I was a little child, I have been familiar with all aspects of doing business. That, combined with babysitting of my sister, did not allow me to have a carefree childhood.

The atmosphere at home was filled with constant stress and fear. Nothing was enough. Nothing was good. Each minor breakthrough was followed by a colossal failure. Everything was constantly wrong. I was wrong, too, no matter what I did or did not do. My dad is a kind man, but he was rarely present mentally and emotionally. All the time, he was on the run to somewhere and not interested in the details of my life. No one asked me personal questions as long as I had the best grades. When I asked for something I needed for my studies or hobbies, my timing was always wrong. Thus since I was sixteen, I frequently took small jobs, which paid roughly $10 per day. Almost nothing was left after I paid for a snack and for transportation. Since it would have taken ages to save up money for my dreams, I used that money to buy snacks for school. At the parties, I would buy a big coke and drink it for the whole night and then walked back home eight kilometers in the middle of the night because I could not afford a taxi, and there were no night trams or busses back then.

In our family, love and money were closely related, and thus I also struggled with them. Money was a great source of stress for me, and I doubted whether I could take care of myself financially. Just like anyone else I knew. This was another family pattern we all shared. During those years, the equation in my subconscious mind was that money broke relationships, and it was a source of constant worry and stress. Subconsciously I also equated loving a guy with hurt, as was the case with Jacob.

But my lessons with love were not over yet. After my seventeenth birthday, I was going out less and less, and I focused on friends rather than on Jacob. One day, I felt that it was finally time to say goodbye to him. We had not seen each other for a couple of months, and then we spent a night together, talking and dancing. That night I decided that it was the last time I saw him. Having one last nice evening without any problems was for me the way to find peace with him and our past. It helped me to close that chapter forever.

Later that year, I met another, improved version of Jacob. Provocatively his nickname was Elvis for his likeness with the king of rock'n'roll. Elvis was six years older, and we met at a bar where he worked evenings as a bartender to support his studies in science. The relationship with Elvis evolved fast, and soon we became an inseparable couple. Unlike Jacob, Elvis kept his word and treated me well. I was happy with him. We never had any issues or arguments, and we laughed a lot together and created some beautiful memories. Meeting Elvis after Jacob was a dream come true, and I found myself in my first committed relationship. I trusted Elvis entirely, and it never even crossed my mind that something could happen when he worked at a bar while I slept at home.

But later into our relationship, I learned from a common friend that there was a woman who visited the bar frequently and talked with Elvis through many nights. That woman was his ex-girlfriend who had left him about half a year before we met. Elvis had mentioned her once, and I assumed that everything was settled between them. My friend also told me that when she learned that Elvis had moved on and was happy with me, she suddenly wanted him back, although she was the one who had left. That is what some women do, and now she targeted me. She would come up with all kinds of stories that later turned out to be untrue to make Elvis feel sorry for not being with her.

After learning this news, I still trusted Elvis and did not even ask him about her. Until one day, when the whole situation escalated, and Elvis told me that he needed a week off to think things over. This was the first time that we talked about his unresolved relationship with his past, and for me, it confirmed what my friend had told me. Although I was shocked, I appreciated his honesty.

That week felt like torture for me. I tried to focus on school and sports, but I could only think of what would come next. I knew that things were out of my control, and although the decision was about me, I could not do anything about it. Finally, after the week was over, we met. During our meeting, I said something that probably was not smart. I told Elvis, "I think that you should try it with her because you will always have doubts if you do not give it a shot. Anyway, she will not stop trying to get you, which will eventually break us."

So we separated peacefully. But as soon as I got home, I realized what I had said, and felt miserable. Unlike before, this end was not planned. My heart shattered, and it took me a couple of months to feel good again. Two months later, I ran into Elvis by accident, and he invited me to spend the New Year's Eve with him and his friends. It felt good as if no time had passed. At that point, he and his ex-girlfriend still did not get back together, but about four months later, they did try it for a while. By then, I had finally moved on as well.

During those years, many things were out of flow in my life. I was unhappy at the grammar school because it felt like working below my level there. Nothing motivated me to study because I had already learned much of the stuff by myself, or I remembered it without any need to review the school material. I could not have a deeper conversation with anyone, and I could sleep during the nights.

My dance with darkness was exhausting, and I needed a breather. For a decade, the strangest things happened during my sleepless nights. When the world became quiet, I experienced everything from the astral plane to curious encounters with all kinds of souls, spirits, ghosts, entities, you name it. As a result, I could not sleep during the nights as something would always wake me up, usually between midnight and three am. Those beings wanted my attention.

Honestly, I did not care what they came to communicate with me, I needed to sleep. I became exhausted as I could not sleep peacefully through a single night. I was irritated with all those beings, and I always sent them away without enquiring why they had come. It was none of my business, I was not a medium after all. I was just a girl who was trying to survive in a stressful home and get through her troubles in love, and I really did not care about any inter-dimensional communications. However, some of those encounters were positive, and those beings taught me some new skills and showed me how to work with energy by using my mind. Although I was not super excited that they needed to come during the night, eventually, I was grateful for my nonphysical teachers.

Still, I was tired every day.

CHAPTER 8

LUKE

A heavy snake curled up on my chest,
Moving rhythmically so I could not flee.
He tightened his body around my breast,
Raising a deadly plea.

My body could not breathe.
The joy stealthy escaped my life.
I start to worry that he may never leave,
Yet, I can tell that I shall not be your wife.

Little by little, death spreads inside,
Like a poison, it wanders my body.
There seems to be nowhere to hide,
Every motion becomes achy.

Go! Find another victim!
No longer, I can walk this path.
Once again, I shall be a pilgrim,
Yet I will never elude your wrath.

Before I went to university, my life took another turn. At the two-hour martial art class that I attended every Monday and Wednesday, I met another man. Luke seemed reasonable and stable. At that point, I was done with the mysterious guys, or so I thought. I needed someone who would not hurt me because the third pain in a row would be too much. I also needed a new circle of my friends because all my friends liked to spend time in pubs, and I did not want to be part of that lifestyle anymore. After the breakup with Elvis, I began to take better care of myself and was gradually uncovering islands of stability within myself. Seeing friends in pubs was one of the first things I quitted after the breakup.

With Luke, I found the kind of stability that my heart had been yearning for. Although our relationship was far from perfect, I could finally rest beside him. Like a cat, I licked my wounds and focused on something else than the survival mode that I had grown up in. Being with Luke marked a critical transition in my life. We moved in only after three months of dating, and I started to study law. Although the law was what my parents had always wanted, I immediately knew that it was a mistake. It felt like in the grammar school where I had lacked any real intellectual challenges. My heart was dissatisfied with memorizing the law codex because with my photogenic memory, it was never an issue. I wished to study something different. Something that would stretch my mind a little.

Luke studied at the University of Economics in Prague, and sometimes I would visit some lectures with him. I liked the way they needed to count and use different parts of their brain, so after a year, I quit the law and passed my entrance exams to the same university. It turned out to be the right decision because I enjoyed the variety of courses. I also took as many optional classes as I could and even those that did not count toward my degree. I would always enjoy learning something new.

In my free time, I would also do yoga, dance salsa, study Japanese, and take piano lessons. But most of all, I would dive into spiritual books. Instead of studying for my final exams, I would always have a stack of spiritual books next to my school notes, and in time it became ever harder for me to focus on economics even though I enjoyed it.

Once again, I felt something new opening up within me. That space felt familiar yet unknown. It rekindled my hunger for knowledge and understanding about the workings of the universe and life within it. I would start counseling some of my friends, and more people would come to ask for guidance. I never said no because helping people brought me a sense of purpose, although often it felt tiring. I would also try to help Luke heal. Back then, I still believed that it was possible to save your partner. After all, I knew what needed to be healed, and I could get him into that space. However, it created inequality in my mind. Suddenly, I did not look up to Luke anymore, and my respect for him was waning.

The time with Luke gradually started to feel like an eternity. It seemed like I was frozen in a movie that would never move onto a new frame. Therefore, I dedicated even more of my focus on spirituality, and I also took random classes just to stay longer at the university where I felt good. However, from the outside perspective, it seemed that I had it all. I knew precisely where I was aiming, what kind of job I was going to get in the business world. And I was engaged to Luke. In 2010, we had been together for more than three years. My life was perfectly lined up. Luke saved me from my family. At least I thought so. He was my savior because, in the beginning, I believed that the old pain was gone, and we could be happy together. For years, I genuinely thought that this was it. All a girl whose heart had been broken by her family and ex-boyfriends could ever dream of. Little did I know that life had again wholly different plans for me.

I believed that Luke loved me sincerely, and I thought I loved him, too. But like for many other people in this world, it was more about my mind loving the idea of being with someone who loved me and cared for me rather than real love. The love I felt did not come from my heart, which I, unfortunately, had not yet recognized. Thus after a couple of years, I began asking myself some challenging questions like, "Would I feel unhappy if this was true love? Would it cross my mind repeatedly that I would be better off alone if we were meant to be together?" These questions were echoing in my mind most of the time.

Luke and I argued frequently, and after every new quarrel, I cared less about our future. I did what I would always do when I was unhappy; I withdrew into myself. All my life, I had sought peace, and as years passed by, it became apparent that we could not have found it together. We both had little experience with relationships, and what we had learned from our parents did not serve us either. My body still stored up stress from the arguments back home, and each time we had a conflict, I went into a panic and wanted to get as far away from him as I could. I would withdraw at least mentally and emotionally. As much as I was hoping to have a beautiful relationship, I could not shake off the fear that my past would eventually catch me. My subconscious mind played on a loop the old story that no matter how much I tried, everything was going to fail eventually. It was a battle that I could not win. Especially when something mattered to me, it seemed to never work out.

Luke himself also had heaps of unhealthy family patterns. It made two of us to do our best to make our relationship work, yet we did not know how. When I was with Luke, I started to believe that it was normal to have issues with your partner. My teenage crushes taught me to anticipate problems and drama. Thus I was caught up in a high-speed train heading toward a destination that I hoped was not going to be my future. Still, I had no evidence of how real love felt, but with each new year, my heart was shouting ever louder: "Leave!"

As my heart was shutting down toward Luke, I felt like dying a slow death. Never before had I felt so empty. I carried a heavy burden from day to day until I could see no light. I will always remember that feeling. I was young, and I had my whole life ahead of me, yet I felt like it was the end. I asked myself every day, "Is this all?" I struggled to see any chance for something better. My life was becoming boxed in. That box had solid and precisely measured edges and borders. Everything was about control. Beside him, I had no idea who I was anymore. Not that I would have known it before, but during our relationship, I got utterly lost. I had lost my connection to myself, to others, and to my life.

As any rational and practical men prefer it, everything in our life had precise structures. Action plans were created. Our life got planned. Every time my soul cried out, "Wake up!" Luke would always offer some well-formed and logical answer to mansplain it away. That experience taught me that it is easy to win someone's mind, but it does not mean that it reaches someone's heart. Everything that he said was only anchored in the logical realm of the mind. While my heart was building up walls against his dominating nature.

Intellectually, I could grasp his rationalizations. Being with Luke offered me a valuable experience to see how logical people think and operate. My brain comprehended his mind's reasoning, but still, all I wanted to do was to shout, "I do not care! Whatever! This is your truth, not mine!

And it never will be! Just leave me in peace! No matter what rational words you use, you can never change the feelings in my heart. They are sacred!"

When one is young, it is easy to misunderstand attention as love. We can misinterpret somebody's act of kindness as a deep-soul interest. At one point, I gave up. And I also learned to filter everything through my mind's eyes, even my own heart. The lines between my heart and mind were blurred, and I confused hell with heaven. Day after day, I was falling deeper in a hole - into a sorrow. That was a tranquil way of dying. Yet, it was more painful. Once you lose hope, nothing truly matters. Nex to Luke, I stopped believing in the dreams I felt that those happy moments that I once felt when I was immersed in studying Egypt could never return.

Luke always cared about external appearance. He wanted to have the best degrees, a perfect career, a beautiful wife, and a spotless life. An older woman who knew both of us once told me that Luke treated me as his doll. He would sit me in a corner, put on a nice dress, and after a while, he would move me somewhere else. With that metaphor, she pointed out what my heart already knew. I happened to be the person who fitted into his idea of a perfect life. He loved to move me from place to place, and I was unable to explain to him that I did not want that. His willpower always exceeded mine, so we ended up doing things the way he wanted.

After four years of this, I stopped utterly caring about what Luke was saying. Confusing whispers reached my ears. Only for the sake of peace, I agreed with anything that he said. Because if I did not agree, he would not leave me until I would have changed my mind based on his wishes. Luke was draining my energy. Everything spun around him, and I felt that there was no space for my true self. My heart yearned for a quiet and secret place where I could be alone, in silence, only me and the divine.

My body felt exhausted, and I needed a lot of sleep, and when the morning came, I did not want to get out of bed because there was nothing to look forward to. Later I found out that my body developed an officially incurable disease, but I knew that it was my body's response to Luke draining my energy. Had I married him, my body would have continued breaking apart because it would have been the only way out - the only possibility to find peace.

During those years, I could not shake off the feeling that I was wasting my life. It was not only about our relationship, but the heavy energy between us also transferred to other areas of my life. I could not move in any direction. The worst of all was that I knew I was walking Luke's path, not mine. I lived his dream that he had for us.

One night, I saw Brona in my dream. She died when I was seventeen and never met either Elvis nor Luke. In the dream, I found myself in a room full of clocks of different sizes. There were dozens of them. Brona stood in front of me and stared intensively into my eyes until I felt uncomfortable. Without using words, Brona told me to wake up and live my path. Then the clocks hit noon, and they all began to ring.

Intuitively, I knew that it was almost too late. Several times in a lifetime, depending on our soul's mission, the doors to a new timeline open. If we hesitate, they close, and we have to wait for another opportunity. Although the universe is patiently teaching us, we usually take the longer path with more detours and obstacles, which eventually lead us to the same destination. Since kindergarten, I was aware of the moments when the door opened, and I also could tell if I had walked through it or allowed my fear to take me on a longer path. Now, the doors were slowly closing, and I could see the future that awaited me if I stayed. It came to me as visions of heavy energy choking me, an unhappy family, and wasted potential before I had another chance to alter the trajectory of my life. Yet, I still felt paralyzed to make a move. I feared his anger and doubted my intuition that guided me to change. As always, I prioritized others over my inner growth and fulfillment.

For a long time, the idea of abandoning Luke felt foreign. I believed in fairy tales. I was programmed to believe in a prince on a white horse who would save me. More importantly, I fell for the illusion that I should stay with the first prince I met for the rest of my life. How many women feel like this? As women, we allow the wrong man to diminish our spark and beauty. After many years in such a relationship, it is hard to start again because it takes time to heal the wounds. Once the self-trust is lost, it takes strong will and determination to regain faith in love.

I did not trust that I could meet anyone else either. At least not a better man. After all, Luke was kind to me, or that was the way I preferred to see him. What else could I wish for? His acts of kindness almost covered the unconscious manipulations. Nothing terrible happened between us, we were just not made for each other. We were trying to make something work that was not meant to be. I believed that struggle was a part of any relationship, and I only needed to find a way to make it work. But what mattered to me even more, was what my dad thought. Unintentionally, he gave me the idea that I should stay with Luke. Those two had a good relationship, and my dad, just like any other dad, wanted his daughter to be protected by someone who would take care of her.

But for such a people-pleaser and a person who would always be afraid to make their own decisions, this became like a written law. How could I go against my dad's opinion? He was never aware of how significantly he influenced me. When my parents looked at my actions, they must have believed that I was a rebel. While on the inside, each of their words and feelings stayed with me for years, shaping the ideas of what was possible for me.

Life enjoys paradoxes. While I could sense the unlimited potential within me, I did not think that someone would ever recognize it, nor could I imagine that I could beat the ill-fortune and tap into it. It was like my secret, entirely hidden in my heart. I knew that I would excel in many things. I was fortunate enough to be good at many things like sports, playing piano, learning languages, or school. But I never kept on with any of these, except for the school.

The reason why I quit everything prematurely was my presupposition that I could not become the best. Not that I would ever feel competitive, luckily, I have never been envious of other people's success. On the contrary, I felt happy and excited for them. But I was competing with my own potential. I saw the gap between where I was and where I could be if I had not stopped trying. And still, my desperate lack of confidence and self-love made me quit one activity after another. Ironically, I would always give them up right before any breakthrough. This happened in sports, as well. From the elementary school, where I attended a special sports class, all the way up to the high school, the sports teachers would always choose me to represent our school at any athletic competition.

Although I won without any other practice than one sports class a week, I never joined a professional athletic team, which I still cherished as a dream for a whole decade.

From outside, my commitment must have seemed questionable, and thus, it was understandable why my parents did not support me in my dream. I cannot blame them for thinking so because I never told them how I truly felt about myself and how much athletics meant to me.

A couple of times, I attempted to tell my dad about how unhappy I was, but he did not believe me. From his perspective, someone like me should not have any reason to doubt themselves. He thought that I was smart, and he knew that I had the best grades from elementary school all the way to the Master's degree at the university. My dad also told me that I was highly ambitious, just like himself, and on top of that, I was beautiful, so why would I ever suffer from low self-confidence? My parents did not see how I cried each night behind the closed doors and how many times it crossed my mind that it would have been better if I did not live at all. My parents could not see how much I longed for their love and a kind word. What was the worth of all talents if you did not feel loved and knew that your existence is important for someone? Love is our nature.

Like any little girl, I needed to hear from my parents how proud they were of me and also that they believed in me. They probably did, but the lack of verbal encouragement made me think that they did not imagine me excelling at anything. So I eventually quit everything. Naturally, I should have done it for myself because I had many passions that made me feel alive. But I did not bother to go all the way when what I was doing seemed invisible to my parents. I lacked faith in me.

For the same reason, I did not leave Luke. I did not believe that I would be fine without him. And what if my dad was right and he was the right partner, after all? I did not dare to risk it to find out. I was seeking approval to follow what my heart already knew. In my past, I was punished for making wrong decisions and especially when I had followed what had felt right for me. "What if I would be punished again?" What if the universe told me after I had left Luke: "What were you thinking, dear Sylvia? Did you really believe that you could finally be happy in your life? Of course, not! Now, you are darned for your daring. You will pay for it forever." Back then, I could not yet distinguish the voice of my ego, so those concerns kept me paralyzed from making the decision to leave.

I was afraid of Luke's anger, and I knew that he would not allow me to leave him. After all, I tried to end our relationship many times. But he never took it seriously. Unfortunately, I do not often shout, so some people question whether I mean what I say. Perhaps if I had yelled at him with all the despair I felt in my heart, he would have let me go. But maybe not.

There seemed to be no way out. Until a holiday in Egypt.

CHAPTER 9

ANGEL

I never anticipated you,
Yet you uncovered your face for me.
How long had I been walking next to your crystal hue?
My sincere prayers were the key.

Your enormous blue eyes
Were nothing like I had ever seen.
Your white starry Light
Is everything I need.

I have found my way to your presence,
Now every pain shall disperse.
But first, we need to mend my Soul's fragments,
Before my human self can traverse.

I can see the ladder to my multidimensional substance.
You are the first of many heralds.
First, all I hear is endless silence,
But, in the distance, I witness emeralds.

Ultimately, the universe heard my prayers and showed me what true love was. It was November 2010, and we set off for our vacation in Egypt. Once again, Egypt was to initiate me into another chapter of my life. This time the tests and trials increased their intensity.

One night we went out with an Egyptian man whom we

had met a few years ago, and we called him familiarly "our brother." It turned out that he now worked right next to our hotel, in a completely different part of the city than the last time we saw him. On our first day, we went to buy a bottle of water in a shop, and we found out that our brother worked there. Luke and I were delighted because we all sensed that we had known each other for ages. I was even more excited because our brother looked like the ancient Egyptians; short, skinny, and with the typically formed facial bones. Nowadays, very few Egyptians possess the original heritage.

One evening, our brother took us to the old part of the city where only locals go. Immediately, we got to participate in an Egyptian wedding, and afterward, we went to eat at a local bistro. By then, I had been in Egypt a couple of times to know well what I could eat without getting the intestinal flu. On my travels, I would never get sick because I was deliberate about food and water. When our brother offered us traditional Egyptian dishes, I instead opted out for a sour-sweet lemon that was supposed to be eaten with the peel. Since it seemed like the least risky thing to eat, I only ate that the whole night. However, Luke was always excited about food and wanted to try everything. So he did, but his stomach did not share Luke's optimism.

Unfortunately for Luke, he got food poisoning, which forced him to stay in a hotel room for almost two weeks. Thus, I went out to a beach alone, and to my surprise, it felt great. I was reading, meditating, and started to open up. To deepen my inner transformation, I took the biggest weapon of mine – a pen. Writing a diary to explore my honest feelings became a haven for me. I did not have anyone else to confide in. This diary, followed by several others, became my best friend.

Almost immediately, I started to experience something that was both new and familiar at the same time. I did not feel abandoned anymore. Something was reaching out to me. Back then, I did not realize that I was revealing a veil to my new existence. Although, now, I understand that I began to build a bridge between myself and my soul. It was somewhere there, in the ancient homeland of the pharaohs, where I first admitted to myself that my life needed to change. More precisely, the relationship with Luke had to shift or come to an end.

And then, one night, I received a vision.

In the vision, I saw a white door in front of me, which I opened. As I pulled the handle, I could see a towering bright angel. His light was shining so powerfully that it almost blinded me. His face was adorned with giant beautiful almond-shaped blue eyes and a loving smile. Standing in front of him felt overpowering. I had a feeling that his light could tear me apart.

He said something that I have never forgotten, "You finally found the way back to me." The light emanating from him was so overwhelming that I nearly started to cry. In all my amazement and shock, I thought, "Thank you, but you have to go, or your bright light will kill me." After a couple of long moments, he disappeared. Perhaps he had more things to tell me, but I was not yet ready to stay in the presence of such intense light. Since that time, I have encountered angels more times. Yet the encounter in Egypt was the harbinger of something new.

After the holiday, when our lives had come back down to earth, I continued talking to my soul. Most of our conversations were initially one-sided as I was praying for help. The walls of our unwelcoming flat mirrored my unhappiness. But the angel gave me hope, and I was determined to change. One way or another. Nevertheless, I was still not the person who would create that change myself. So, I prayed and hoped that the change would occur differently - from the outside.

One night, I prayed to my soul to either bring into my life the person I was meant to be with or to change the relationship with Luke and help me to love him. Finally, I made a decision that I could not stay trapped between the two worlds. Living that way was leading nowhere. I asked my soul to reveal my path and to send me to my other half. In my prayers, I wished to meet someone so close that I could read his mind, and he could read mine. I wanted to meet the one I had belonged to since the beginning of time. Like any woman, I just asked for the perfect love - nothing more and nothing less. My awareness of his existence was increasing every day.

A few weeks later, Luke came home and excitedly told me about a guy I had to meet. "He is exactly like you. I know you will get along very well. I have a strong feeling that you really have to get to know him," he repeated. "When I was talking with him, it was like being with you. You even have the same gaze in your eyes." Luke seemed overly enthusiastic, and he was determined to introduce us to one another.

Although I had his phone number for several months, I still postponed contacting him. There was no rational reason for my hesitancy, which was coupled with deep and undefined fear. One late February afternoon, when I was on a bus to visit my parents, I found the courage to text him. The reply came almost instantly. He replied with a nice and long message. While I read the message, my heart was shaking as if the secrets of the universe were hidden there.

Maybe they were. I, for sure, had opened Pandora's box.

CHAPTER 10

THE ENCOUNTER

The tears dripped down my face,
Like golden pearls cascading my cheeks.
Their smoothness is of exquisite lace,
Their omen is mystique.

How many lifetimes have you been here?
How many lifetimes have you intertwined with me?
Now, you come into my life like a flurry of air
To unravel the lost diamond key.

When a mist covered my eyes, I saw you coming.
First, your lips kissed mine in dreams.
The angels announced the novelty you bring,
My tears formed powerful streams.

A black thrush woke me up that morning,
Transformed my heart into a white flower,
Prophesying the times of deep mourning.
My lips whispered, "please, be my lover."

I recognized my imprint in you,
Your eyes mirrored back my soul.
Our soul bodies united before we knew,
We courageously stepped into our new role.

It was a Tuesday morning of early spring in Prague when I

was waiting in front of an old coffee place. Nervous. Excited. Not understanding why I felt that way made me even more jittery. "What is about to happen? Why do I feel like my heart wants to jump out of my body?" These were my only thoughts that bright cold morning while waiting for him to come.

I was gazing in a shop window when, all of a sudden, my body shivered. I looked over my shoulder, and our eyes first met. For a few seconds, a deep eye connection penetrated our souls. We both began to smile and hug. He seemed nervous, too. But soon we started to talk like we had known each other forever. Perhaps we did. There are a few souls with whom I feel particularly close, including my sister and dad. But I had rarely felt this with a stranger. Certainly not with such intensity. There was just one question echoing in my head, "Where have you been all my life?" It felt like we were born for each other.

When we sat down, he asked me to tell him something about myself. This is a tricky question that I struggle with even today. I am never sure what the correct answer is. All I want to say is, "I just am. I feel. I breathe. I exist." From my perspective, this is the most precise answer, but it appears to confuse others. But I did my best that morning and replied, "I am Sylvia, and I have astral plane dreams where I can travel anywhere. But they are also terrifying because I am not in control of them. They just happen to me." He was looking at me for a little while, probably thinking whether I truly just said what he had heard, and then he asked me, "How do you get to the astral plane?"

"I do not try to get there. I am not sure why, but I simply go there most nights, and I see strange creatures." Yes, this was the way I nicely and quite plainly introduced myself. 'This went well," I thought, "I think I sounded normal. It was surely better than just replying that I am," I was satisfied with my answer. This set the tone for the course of our future discussions, and we dealt with it with grace, curiosity, and laughter. Talking with him felt natural because I could share my weirdness openly, and he did not seem to be frightened by it. That is at least what I thought.

I was delighted when I realized that he was curious about all the topics between heaven and earth. Until that point, I had guarded this part of myself against others. Most of my friends had no idea what I was interested in. They did not know about it because I was too scared to appear that I was too out of the box. Which I certainly would have in the small industrial town I grew up in. For some reason, I sensed that I could share all this with the person I had just met. Since I had always felt like an alien among others, I felt comforted by the fact that there were at least two of us.

Undoubtedly, there was a strong magnetism between us. We had many similar stories, feelings, and ways of looking at the world. Our conversation flowed naturally, and it felt like talking with my own soul. Something perfectly clicked, and we were on the same vibe. I remember sitting in that old coffee place and feeling a bit dizzy. For a few hours, my whole life became surreal. When we were looking into each other's eyes, it felt like all my experiences had led me to that very moment. Time collapsed. At one point, I felt that this had already happened as if we were re-experiencing our past. At the same time, I felt like I had accidentally visited my future or perhaps a parallel reality. Then time stopped, and I did not realize that a quick coffee turned into some more, a lunch, and then several more hours until the late afternoon.

Before we separated, it was clear to me that I had unearthed something unknown. My heart was wide open, and my body felt hot, burning with a thousand degrees. All these feelings and sensations were new to me. "What has just happened?" I pondered on my way home, back to Luke. There was a bright glow around me that surely even a blind person would see. But Luke did not. He failed to notice anything strange about me.

This was exactly what was different about Luke; he was not open to spirituality the way I was. And I was not as much into practical things as he was. In a span of years, the gap between us had grown wider, until it was clear that he did not understand me anymore. He only saw his idea of who I was, but my true self stayed invisible to him.

When I got to the student dorms, where we lived back then, Luke only worried about why I stayed so long. "Do I know?" I asked myself. I had been taken into another reality, and my mind was clueless. It could not comprehend the intensity of my feelings. It was like my whole body, heart, and soul had awakened. From the very moment, I knew that I had changed forever. My mind could not comprehend why I felt so close to someone I had never before met. Close on a different level. Nothing made sense even though it did. That day, I understood that no meetings are accidental.

Eventually, Luke could feel that the aura around me had transfigured. In my life, meeting Kahl was the brightest, most exciting, and mysterious moment yet. I felt like I was born only for that moment. I was so grateful for knowing that someone like him existed. Kahl's existence brought me peace, excitement, and a new zest for life.

It took me a couple of months to admit that I had fallen in love with Kahl. As well as to concede that I was petrified, not knowing where it would lead. I had no idea how to tell Luke. Yet, I knew that another way of living existed. My soul had answered my call for help. Finally, I was confident that I did not want the kind of life that I had been living. And I sensed that our encounter was only the beginning. For me, living between the old and new world was the hardest part. It was excruciating to still have to live your old life, while you already knew that you do not belong there anymore. Yet you do not have enough courage to make that jump. The hesitation with indecision is the worst. And I tended to hesitate.

It takes time for the mind and heart to find alignment. Sometimes, it takes years for the perception to shift. Other people might say, "Yes, you are right; there is more to life, but think about your children, your commitments, your job...' This one little 'but' is devilish. It kills the courage. It poisons the excitement, and you begin to doubt the heart's gentle intelligence.

While levitating somewhere between the two worlds, you do not belong anywhere. Your gut sense is shouting, "Just make the jump, it is going to be fine," but you cannot trust it. How could you when your heart has been bruised so many times? You wish your senses were right, but you think that these beautiful things do not happen to you. Maybe if you had been brought up in an encouraging environment, it would be simpler, or perhaps not. But what if you had not received the support you needed? What then? What if no one else has seen the real beauty of your soul yet?

We, humans, have a special gift to quieten the voice of our heart. We wait in silent misery until the voice leaves us. Then, we start seeking comfort from the outside. We deny our inner power and continue to stay stuck. Stuck in self-accusations and indecision. This is a vicious circle.

It was a rollercoaster of feelings around the time I met

Kahl. My feelings were blended with guilt because I was with Luke. While on the other hand, in the light of my feelings toward Kahl, I had to admit to myself the fact that I was trying to suppress – I was not going to spend the rest of my life with Luke. I liked him, and I was doing my best to make our relationship work. But my feelings for him were nothing near to what I felt for Kahl. That led to another realization; before I met Kahl, I did not know what love was. Little did I know about the true capacity of my heart to love when I was praying to experience it. Our encounter shook me entirely, and I was not willing to admit my feelings to myself. For if I had, I would not only have left Luke, but I would also have had to change the direction of my life.

As my heart was awakening, I started to realize that I was living in a land built on lies. This applied not only for my relationship but also for what I had studied and who I had told myself I was. My heart was whispering to me that my perception of myself was limited and that it was time for a transformation. My life began to gain a new spark and purpose. This encounter initiated the awakening of my soul in my human body. I was waking up from a very long and bad dream. And I had no logical way to explain the connection I felt with Kahl.

The heavens and earth had shifted.

CHAPTER 11

KAHL

The dark rose kissed my lips,
A ruby dragon wrapped around my hips.
I know this is the dimming,
There is no more of what I must.

The edges broke down,
The spirits lay down,
Stealthily into my bed,
Creating around me a web.

I got trapped,
While my heart cracked
Wide open,
Into the vast ocean.

Hear the whispers,
Hear the songs.
All the sorrow shall not be gone!
It shall sing me its song.

Slowly into my ears
Until I could nothing but understand.
While the clouds shattered my mind
And the whole world soaked into the night.

Until everything vanishes out of my sight;
Please, stay and hold me tight.

I am your mistress; I am your love.
We have forfeited, far from the light.

Kahl and I met again the following week and the week after. Our meetings provoked the same intensive feelings in me. During each of our encounters, we spent long hours of sharing, opening, and sinking into each other. Together with my heart opening to him, I unlocked an unrecognized power within myself to cope with anything. With the pure knowledge that he existed; all the problems felt insignificant.

The laughter and joy returned to my life. I once again began to experience heightened spiritual dreams and visions which had been absent during my years with Luke. Kahl was my sweet secret. I was not alone anymore, but there was also him as well, a wild, spontaneous, and sincere man. Nobody else touched my inner realms as deep as Kahl. He unlocked the unknown dimensions of my heart and soul. Meeting him was the moment when I returned to spirituality with full commitment. Piece by piece, I established the bridge to my soul. There was not only passion and love, but, more importantly, there was a deeply spiritual bond.

Nevertheless, I was transfixed with a painful dilemma about what to do next. There was nothing physical between Kahl and me, yet I felt like I was cheating. Perhaps at the soul level where Luke, unfortunately, had never reached, I was. My mind was constantly trying to solve this dilemma. On the one hand, there was a commitment to Luke that was weighing me down. On the other hand, my heart had started beating with a renewed thrill for life again.

What was the right choice? Fear or my freedom? I was

consumed with the fear of the unknown. I was thinking, "If I break up with Luke, what will I do next? What kind of person would I become?" More doubts came in, "What would I tell my family and friends? They will judge me because I would disappoint them."

"On the other hand, I cannot fight the magnetic power pulling to Kahl. But, what if he is as scared as I am? What if neither of us is ready for the intensity that exists between us?" These thoughts were running in my mind on a repeat. After what felt like an eternity, my fears covered my mind, and a sense of morality won at last. I wanted to do the right thing and stay committed to Luke, although it was breaking my heart.

It was a dark and rainy April afternoon when I sent Kahl away unintentionally. We met in a coffee place near his flat, and I could feel how out of sync we both were that morning. As we sat by the small table facing each other, Kahl grabbed my hand and asked, "Why are you wearing the engagement ring today?" I rarely wore the ring Luke gave me last summer because it felt uncomfortable. Moreover, our engagement was secret, and our families did not know about it because we had not planned to get married for another couple of years anyway. Although I had not worn the ring intentionally that day, it reminded Kahl that I was not as free as he wished I were. He seemed immersed in his thoughts for a moment, and then he continued, "You have a boyfriend, family, friends, and what about me? Where do I belong in your life?"

His words hurt me. I knew that I would not be able to resist if he ever fought for me. But he would not do it because he was full of doubts, and he feared our genuine soul-to-soul connection. Intuitively, already, when we met for the second time, I knew that he was not going to fight for me - for us. I knew that it all depended on me. It was a dangerous combination. I had my own fears, too, and I needed reassurance just like him. After some hesitation, I said, "I am sorry if you do not feel like you belong in my life, Kahl. I wish you would. And I know you do. You just do not want to admit it to yourself. Maybe, I do not want to admit it either. But I will marry Luke. I promised it to him, and I will keep my word..."

I continued talking, but the words escaping my mouth were plain, lacking any depth or truth. We both sensed it. I wanted to persuade myself into thinking that I had made the right choice. Yet, as soon as I said it out loud, I knew it was a lie, and I instantly regretted it. However, it was a more challenging thing to admit out loud what I truly felt. I needed him to help me. And I think that he needed me to help him. In the end, we both ended up locked in our own worlds, unable to reach out to one another.

The fact that Kahl also had his own baggage of pain and patterns did not benefit our situation. I sensed that Kahl did not feel worthy of love. He had stopped believing in true love, and perhaps unconsciously, he did not trust women. He believed that the people he loved and cared about always had to abandon him. Well, that one, we both had in common, so no wonder we left each other. This is the power of patterns when we allow them to rule our lives.

The patterns work this way: two people trigger each other's fears and weak spots. One unintentionally reminds their partner of the past hurts that rarely has something in common with the present situation. In this manner, it continues until they both build a protective wall between them. As a reaction to that thickening wall, they both unconsciously close their hearts to save themselves from any additional pain. When the patterns are playing out, both mistakenly believe that it is the other person hurting them, while all along, they dread to face their own demons. Even if the two people are perfect for each other, they do not see it. Since the only loud and tangible reality is the fearful voice at the back of the head. They hesitate until it is too late.

Our case was not exceptional, we were not immune to our patterns either. At some point, it was clear that we were both locked in our little prisons with the walls made of wrong perceptions and intense fears. Unable to reach the other, Kahl left the coffee shop and told me that he was not going to see me again.

That was it.

Somewhere deep within me, I needed Kahl's encouragement and his faith in us. Perhaps that was the subconscious reason for telling him how determined I was to marry Luke. In reality, I needed to hear, "I love you. You are worth waiting for. We will figure out everything. We will be fine. Do not worry about anything now. We are together, and nothing else matters. I have never felt anything so deep for anyone in my life and, although it might not be easy, we will be fine." If he had said anything like that, I would have left Luke that very same day.

But, instead, our fears crept in, and I watched him walking away from me. Leaving me standing there alone with my tears.

After that rainy April morning, I once again turned to my logical side for rescue. What happened with Kahl hurt so much that my life lacked a sense of purpose. I felt wholly dead inside. I decided to put all my energy into finishing my studies. I shut down my heart and all my feelings. Nothing mattered to me. I was like a walking zombie. There was no reason to laugh. Even when I talked with my kindred spirit, my sister, I could not have laughed. This was very unlike me.

Life did not hold back from sending me more pain as my family beloved dog had an unexpected heart attack and passed away in front of my eyes. Bono's big body and his small heart could not cope with the scorching weather that summer. Days with Luke felt emptier than ever. It started to be evident that not even my determination could ever fix our relationship. That taught me a valuable lesson, which is not meant for you, cannot be mended.

Moreover, a family member got seriously ill. I wanted to support her and come closer to her, but the opposite happened. As usual, I got the blame for her disease and for everything else only because I was different. Simply, and sadly, everything went wrong.

Under the weight of my unbearable feelings, I decided to talk with Luke about us. It was summer afternoon when I gathered my strength to tell him about Kahl. "Luke, there is something I need to tell you. I love Kahl. I have loved him since the very first moment we met. I did not cheat on you, but my feelings belong to him. I am so sorry. I really wanted things to work out between us." I could not hold it inside me any longer. Even though there had not been any contact between Kahl and me for a couple of weeks, I finally said it out loud for myself.

He seemed shocked. Luke had sensed that something was going on but never thought that I would fall in love with Kahl. "I cannot believe it. I should not have introduced you to each other. I am such an idiot." He shouted, justly, at me. I hoped that this would be a good enough reason for him to let me go. After many unsuccessful attempts to leave Luke, I did not see any other way out of the relationship than admitting my feelings for Kahl.

However, Luke surprised me. A few hours later, he came to me and said, "It will be ok. You will get over it. We will continue with our plans." His words were like a sharp knife into my heart. "Do you not get it? I cannot move on. I love someone else. It cannot be planned and solved as some equation. There is nothing to get over," I could not believe his words. On the other hand, his response was very much like him. In his world, I was like a puppet that he could maneuver wherever he wanted.

Still, I was captured somewhere in between the two worlds. The jump to a new world was very slow and painful. Instead of jumping, I was crawling with the rest of my energies. My heart was full of pain gathered from failed relationships, broken heart, my loveless childhood, and from not following my heart and do something meaningful with my life.

One day, after many arguments, Luke eventually got it. In a weak moment of upset, he said that we should break up. I immediately saw a unique opportunity and agreed. I started to build my life from scratch.

A few weeks later, I found the strength to contact Kahl again.

CHAPTER 12

SUMMER PROMISES

Too many excuses, too many lies,
There was no future, no light.
All tears already dried up,
It was too long during the dark night.

You have always been lost.
You have never known what you wanted.
Staying close to you would mean too big of a cost.
All your promises were clouded.

It is time to take your promises back.
Sometimes they feel like a curated piece of art.
Now I know that I shall be safely led
To a new home within my heart.

"Hey, Kahl. I hope you are great. We have not seen each other for a long time. Would you like to grab a coffee someday?" I texted him even though this move felt like a teasing snake with my bare feet. But I needed to do it for myself. I still felt guilty for how things had turned out between Kahl and me, and I wanted to buy myself inner peace by knowing that I did my best. Somewhere deep within, I was hoping that we two could get a fresh start. This time without any other commitments from my side so that we would have an honest chance to see whether our relationship could work. Naturally, I had to try because there was not a day that would pass without me regretting sending Kahl away.

It did not take long before I got a text from him saying: "Hey Syl. Nice to hear from you. I am sorry for how I reacted when I last saw you. I feel embarrassed. Coffee sounds good."

We met later that week, and I was even more nervous than the last time because I wanted to know where we now stood. I had not seen him for some time, so I was not sure what had changed. Luckily, the conversation felt natural between us. Like no time have had passed. We discussed our life plans, travel plans, and what had happened since our last encounter. We found out that our dreams did change yet in a similar manner. As we discussed our dreams, I realized that living without following my purpose was becoming more painful than staying in the comfort zone. I have always wanted to have a partner-in-crime. A powerhouse partnership where both of us are 100 percent individuals with a strong sense of life mission, and we also support each other and create beautiful synergy. My vision was to have each other's back so that our potential would skyrocket as a result of the soul connection. Intuitively, I knew that having a relationship with Kahl would mean embracing my potential. There was no way that we could have a traditional relationship, I was certain that we would always inspire each other to grow beyond what we thought was possible.

The question remained - were we ready for this? Was I ready?

When Kahl looked into my eyes, I felt him at the bottom of my soul. It was an unexplainable deep connection. This had not changed. Yet it seemed that something was preoccupying his mind. Kahl asked painstakingly about Luke. With a sense of relief, I answered that we broke up, and I was free. This news surprised Kahl. Yet, against my hope, he did not hug me. Something had changed. We were as close to each other as ever before, yet so far away. I could not stop pondering what was wrong. But for that answer, I still needed to wait a half a year longer.

"Would you come to my place? We can enjoy the sunset on the balcony together," Kahl's question ripped me away from my thoughts. "I would love that," I replied. He continued surprising me even more. As we were already enjoying the sunset, Kahl told me, "I am going to NYC next month, and I would love you to come with me." By coincidence, I had also planned to go there around the same time without knowing about his plans. "I am also going to NYC," I replied. "Actually, next month as well. We might go together then. It would be nice," my voice was shaking.

Even though I agreed, I could not imagine how it would be. Us, in early autumn, NYC with so many unspoken and unlived dreams. No matter what Kahl said, I could not shake off an overwhelming feeling that we could not be together. There was a big fear hanging in the air between us. We were both insecure and scared. Neither of us understood precisely why, but it was louder than any words.

Yet when I was looking into Kahl's eyes, the doubts disappeared for a moment. For a while, everything felt right. Why did I see the stars in his eyes? Why could I read his mind? Why did I have a connection with him that was different from anything else I had ever felt? For unexplainable reasons, I felt a lot of pain whenever I thought about Kahl. My family patterns and self-doubts rushed to the surface and brushed me off with their intensity. It made me rethink the meaning of my past life. Who was I? Where did I want to go? Everything that used to make sense turned upside down. Not just once, but multiple times.

Kahl felt the same way, I believe. I was not surprised when he told me, "Syl, I feel such a deep connection with you. So deep that it scares me. It is like I have always known you. Yet you seem so distant. So far away. At a place where I cannot reach you," Kahl described what we both knew. "What are you afraid of, Kahl? What is the worst thing that could happen if we were together?" I startled myself with what I just said. I was not all that sure if I wanted to hear the answer. Also, it felt unfair to ask him that question since I had the same fears, and I was not able to understand myself. Maybe he could make some sense out of it for both us.

It was clear that answering those questions was not easy for him either. "I feel that if we were together, it would be something special and big. Bigger than anything else until now. I could achieve anything with you. We would become limitless together. We are like two strong magnets pulling each other together. Yet, there is also something deeper pushing us apart," Kahl replied. "But why are you so afraid?" I still insisted. "With you, Syl, I could become the man of my dreams. You are mysterious, intelligent, and beautiful. You seem to have it all figured out," Kahl answered. "This is not true, Kahl. Trust me, I have not figured it out. Actually, not even close to it," I replied.

Unfortunately, any explaining was futile. We were both dragged into our own isolated worlds. A wall of separation was growing thicker and thicker. We felt disconnected from each other and drawn into our own minds. Subconsciously I understood that it would not have worked out between us because of our illusions and fears. No different reasoning was required.

On top of that, I knew that Kahl did not feel worthy of me, and that knowledge drove me crazy. I saw myself as someone above him, but there were no words to explain to him that it was a mere illusion in his own mind. Perhaps, I was more spiritually connected, but I had my fair dose of fears and limiting beliefs, too. They were stopping me just like him. Back then, I did not know that not feeling worthy of someone while putting them on a pedestal with the same breath, is one of the master tools of the ego to deny love.

How could you be with someone you feel such an inexplicable connection with when you feel like you cannot reach them? When you feel like you do not belong to their world? In my mind, he belonged to me more than anyone else. But how could I have ever explained it to him when the fears blurred his vision?

All the words would fall short when the fears took over his hearing. I felt saddened that he did not recognize my true self. I wanted him to see the true me, which is limitless, but also human, both at the same time. Could he have grasped how much unconditional love I carried for him within my heart? When I looked at him, I saw no flaws. For I was looking past them, deep into his soul. Is it not the greatest gift of all to meet your soul-sister who can see the beauty in you that you are not yet ready to recognize? He would think that I did not know his true self, but he did not know that I could see past what he could not have seen.

Kahl's presence revealed to me the gift of seeing the soul of people while looking into their eyes or feeling into their energetic field. Kahl was the first person I could meet at the deep soul level, and there I saw myself too. Our deep bond originated from our souls being close to each other. I sensed that our paths would come apart, but I also felt confident that no amount of years passing by, our connection would always remain strong.

When I walked away from his apartment, my heart shattered into a million pieces. I felt empty. Hopeless. Guideless. Meaningless. I knew that it was the end. At least for now.

CHAPTER 13

FROM THE BOTTOM UP

A golden dagger ripped through my heart,
Fire chariots spread it apart.
The days turned into long nights.
Heavy winds blew off the lights.

When the precious is taken from my life,
All I can do is to feel dead inside.
Life lacks a touch of shine,
I need to become my own bride.

Where should I go?
God, where do you send me?
My soul shouts a big no,
Yet, there is no one around me.

Help me to see the wisdom that dwells within,
The edge between sorrow and love is sometimes so thin.
I was blind to see the truth.
The Universe, please, return me my youth.

Months passed by, and we met a couple times, but we never made it to NYC together. We both visited the Big Apple, but separately. I could not travel because I needed to finish my bachelor's degree, and until the last moment, I did not know the dates of my final exams. After the summer, we were not in contact again. I hit rock bottom again. Looking backward, this was one of the darkest periods of my life. I felt disconnected from life. From friends, school, family, and even my hobbies. I was walking in a grey valley of despair. By Christmas, I thought it could not get any worse, so I contacted Kahl.

Perhaps, it was the same mistake again. Sometimes, it is difficult to accept what is. We fight against it. We see that there is no future, no meaning, nothing, yet we still contact them again. We do not want to trust our gut feelings. Maybe, I was naïve to contact Kahl again. Maybe I did not yet know life so well. For whatever reason, I decided to jump into the pain again, instead of investing in a new life undefined by Luke or Kahl.

We met shortly after Christmas. I took all my courage and decided to open up. Completely. No pretending. No illusions. Just me this time. The truth was that I secretly hoped that things still could change for the better. A spark of hope was alive. But most of all, I wanted to understand why my feelings toward him did not change. "What was our connection about?" I kept asking myself.

However, things turned out far from what I had hoped for. We started talking like two strangers in that dark pub. "How have you been? And how was your trip to NYC?" I asked. Kahl had spoken for about an hour or so when he stopped and looked at me saying, "Syl, did you want to talk about NYC?" "Not really," I admitted. "I have to tell you something, Syl," Kahl said, and my breath stopped. "I met someone. A girl who became my girlfriend..." As I later found out, he was already with her in the summer when we still met a couple of times.

He continued talking excitedly about her. While, for me, it was like the whole world had stopped. The sentences escaping his lips sounded blurry and distant. I saw his mouth opening but could not hear any words coming out. I wanted to shout, "Do not you realize how much it hurts? Can you see that I love you and my heart is bleeding right now? How can you be so insensitive and blind to my feelings? Do I mean nothing to you?" But I did not dare to say anything. Once again, I swallowed my truth and let him dig deeper into my wounded heart with a sharp knife. I did not tell him that I did not need to know how great she was. Of course, she must have been, but talking about her felt so surreal. It felt so wrong. It made it all too real.

My heart was beating fast. My palms got sweaty. My world lost its meaning. The only thing I was thinking about was how to get out of there as quickly as possible. After we parted, an unstoppable waterfall of tears began. I did not remember how I got home. While undressing from the sexy red dress that I bought for our meeting and removing my makeup, suddenly, a wave of anger arose. I got upset with my parents for not supporting me. Had I received the support, I would have known how to deal with this situation. Or even better, I would have not gotten there in the first place. Somehow my sense of worth and self-love were related to what had happened.

My mind flooded me with one thought after another. I thought that if my parents had shown me their love, I would have found love within myself, and would not have chosen to contact Kahl again. Then I got upset with my brother, whom my parents always preferred. Why him? Why was such unequal treatment needed in the first place? I was also upset with Luke, who was killing me slowly and holding me trapped in his nest. Then I got angry with myself for studying at the university where Luke had brought me. Although I enjoyed business, having a business degree was not my soul's calling. Instead, I always wanted to study

Egyptology, quantum physics, or astrophysics. But once again, as seemed to be a pattern for me, my surroundings persuaded me that I would not make a living with any of those degrees. They brought it even a step further by making it clear that I would disappoint them, and they would not support me financially at all if I chose something else. My dad said that I could study the universe or Egypt as a hobby one day after I had become a successful business consultant or a lawyer - the only two options I could consider. As if I had an unlimited amount of time and energy. I was furious for getting further away from my dreams with all those decisions I made.

But my anger did not stop just there, I was angry for waiting my whole life to get recognized. For someone to reach out a helping hand. I was angry for being too kind and too polite. For always saying, "It is ok, I will be fine, it does not matter," when it *did* matter. That night, my life seemed like a pointless joke to me. A wave of regret swept me, and I tasted the pain of not following my dreams. For holding myself back because I was more concerned about my surroundings than myself. I feared the anger of people close to me because they liked to display hard emotions on every occasion. But the biggest pain of them all, even greater than the pain I felt because of Kahl, was because I did not follow my potential. That night I realized that I always followed the path which others had prepared for me, and I could not have ended up more unhappy. It was insane, I could not continue walking this path a minute longer. No energy was left in me to keep other people satisfied.

It became evident that things needed to change rapidly. I needed to change, and thus I decided to leave the Czech Republic. I needed a fresh beginning somewhere I did not have to fear to bounce into Kahl by accident. This time I needed the new start just for myself. So after my first year of the master's program, I passed the entrance exams and went to study a double master's degree in International Trade in China and Belgium. Although I could have stayed in the same country as everyone I knew, it was not an option for me. There were no reasons to remain, just painful memories wherever I looked.

I desired to find a new home as far away as possible. China sounded like a good choice. Even more so since I did not know anything about that country back then. So, I packed a suitcase and opened a new door in my life. Later, it showed up to be the best choice I could have made. Being so far from everything familiar provided me with space to rethink my life and to gain insight. China offered me a warm home. It provided me with a sacred place to heal from my past wounds. China became my new family. My new lover. My new hope.

CHAPTER 14

MY CHINESE LIFE

A golden red dragon hugged me,
And exclaimed, "No more fire!
No more tears!
I shall be your guide!"

A glow wrapped around me,
Bright as the morning mist.
The dragon foretold that I shall be saved,
Now the nightmares are long gone.

His tail lifted me above the clouds,
Lovingly holding me tight,
Into the promised land,
Into the land of the stars.

He recognized my power,
The inherited strength.
The Eastern Star became my anchor,
Wiring me into the cosmic wavelength.

The Serpent reminded me of my origin,
He ignited the sign of my calling;
I shall follow his lead out of the famine
As one of his kind.

He brought me peace.
He evoked a new life.

There,
In the land of the stars!

The greatest thing about China was that I did not know anything about that beautiful country except that the capital is Beijing. Before moving, I did not even check the map. Sorting out the details before traveling has never been among my top priorities. I had no idea where my new home, called Xiamen, would be. Did it really matter? It was enough that it was unknown and afar. It is refreshing to come to a new place without any prejudices. In China, I was open to everything. My sad eyes metamorphosed into the curious eyes of a child. My yearning for growth reawakened.

First, I flew to Shanghai, where the speed of life is faster than down south. Everything and everyone is in constant motion. It was immediately apparent that I had come to a new-old world. There were not many foreigners in China back then. If you saw a foreigner, you were surprised and did not take it for granted. Locals usually do not speak any English at all. The signs are in Chinese, so even if you stand in front of the building you were looking for, you have no clue whether this is the right place. You cannot ask anyone unless you speak Mandarin, or you get lucky and find some foreigner who is less lost than you.

Another unusual occurrence was "the smell of Shanghai." The whole city was pervaded by an omnipresent smell of burned engine oil; at least I suppose that it was oil. I have never smelled anything so disgusting. To be fair, some of my friends were not honored by this unforgettable odor. Maybe I just got lucky that early September week in 2012. But all of this belonged to the excitement. Everything was a harbinger of the novelty ahead of me. After I had learned how to eat rice with the chopsticks, another challenge came – the soup with long thick, slippery noodles.

I liked to be invisible in a room of strangers, but now I earned the attention of all my new classmates at the welcoming dinner because I was unable to feed myself with the chopsticks. For a vegetarian, the noodle soup was the only option, and frankly, I did not know how challenging it would be for a chopstick newbie like myself. The noodle soup turned into a tough challenge, and I was losing the battle. Until a guy whom I had recently met and who studied a different field took pity on me and fed me. That was a lovely way to make an impression. China can teach you a lot.

As it turned out, Xiamen was the perfect city for me to live in. It is an island connected to the mainland with tunnels and bridges. The eastern part of Xiamen faces the island of Taiwan. For me, there was everything I could have wanted. Beautiful hills with various kinds of trees and flowers, parks, and greenness every few hundred meters. Lakes, beaches, and paths for jogging. And our fantastic university campus.

The Chinese architecture honors the principles of Feng Shui, so everything is spacious and well-thought-out. The university campus has two athletic stadiums, a big lake with palm trees and benches to sit and observe the wild geese, tea houses, and shops. There are a few gates from and into the campus, one to the beach, another through a hill to the other side, and the third to a Buddhist temple, Nanputuo. Xiamen provided me plenty of new things to explore each day. One could not get bored there. Nevertheless, as I found out, people either love or hate China. There is nothing in between.

It is all about acceptance. The western way of living and expecting things to unfold smoothly seems to be a useless approach there. Forget it. The Chinese people operate on a different vibration. You have to attune yourself to their wavelength, or otherwise, thousands of tiny contrasts drive you crazy. For me, tuning in showed up to be an easy task. The acceptance enabled me to meet the real China. I allowed China to reveal its magic to me, and I soaked it all in.

China taught me to enhance endurance. To stroll slowly and feel my steps. To get up early and watch the sunrise. To savor the sunsets from a beach or a hill. To get connected with Buddha in the fascinating temples devoted to him. People come to temples to pray and burn incense every day. One can feel their prayers and blessings hovering in the air. Many times, I went to the Nanputuo temple alone to sit down, close my eyes, and simply feel. My meditations in the overcrowded temple usually took half an hour or longer.

Peace and balance would instantly take over my mind and heart. Sometimes, these sacred moments moved me so strongly that I could not help but cry. However, the temples can be bustling places, it did not matter. It has a unique charm when you cannot understand the local language. What people around you are saying becomes only a stable and distant sound to you. You become an observer. Not too close to get involved, but not too far that you would not feel the culture.

These temple moments have stayed in my heart ever since. By recalling those memories, I can re-experience the calm, peace, and balance. That was my sweet secret. When friends asked me where I disappeared, I knew that going to the Nanputuo temple by the campus was not what they had expected. They were right - it was not the correct answer. I entered an unfamiliar space. My body was sitting in the lotus position, while my mind and heart joined Buddha.

Time flew differently in China. In two years, I lived a few distinctive lives. Every day was filled with countless fresh experiences. Thus it did not feel like two years had passed, but rather like ten years. I was becoming a child again. A fearless, spontaneous, and happy child.

CHAPTER 15

DANGEROUS COMPANIONS

You came as a friend,
As a kindred soul,
Smiling and whistling,
As a sign of an upcoming show.

What happened to you, my dear friend?
The shadows covered your sight,
Illusions covered your mind,
I do not recognize you anymore.

Where did you go?
Where did you disappear?
Perhaps, a black mage
Kidnapped your soul.

The illusion creeps in slowly,
Not revealing its true self.
Yet, it is time to get clear
And regain yourself.

Dear friend, I do not know you anymore.
What has become of your heart?
Yet from afar, I hear you roar.
May the angels guide you home.

I enjoyed my international trade classes a lot. It was an

interesting experience to study in a class with Chinese Ph.D. students who studied nonstop, and none of us could compete with their dedication. I got the impression that they memorized every textbook by heart. Often, I would see them leaving the school library before it closed at eleven o'clock at night to show up early the next morning again. For various reasons, partly as an experiment, I happened to be in the same class as them. Yet, Chinese and Western students had varying backgrounds and interests in international trade. Although the courses were new to me, I had the advantage of having already studied most of the material in my previous master's degree. So I did not need to spend too much extra time to understand complex computations.

My days were grounded in a positive routine. Finally, I started to pay attention to some new things other than Kahl or Luke. We did not have much free time, but when there was, I would travel. China is a vast country, and although I visited many places, I still could not explore the whole country. On the other hand, it is always good to have some reasons to return.

After a couple of years of living in the dorms, I wanted more space and decided to find an apartment. There was a group of other Czech students who studied the same program, so we decided to share a flat together. It was more an act of convenience than friendship. Each of us had distinct characteristics that made it difficult for us to bond. Some girls were going to school and coming back, without any desire to explore China and Chinese culture. They seemed to be busy gossiping about others after school. While others were living in their own universes, which were challenging for the rest of us to understand.

But there was one girl, Kathy, who caught my attention.

When you like someone or when someone is abusive to you, you are attracted to them by the same intensity. It might be challenging to tell whether a friendship is beneficial or whether you are magnetized by the negative karma. Everything related to Kathy was one big lesson for me. At first, I did not resonate with her. My very first impression of her was, "Watch out! There is something strange and dark about her." Although my instincts guided me against her, I also felt sorry for her as the others did not seem to like her. So once again, I chose to ignore my gut feelings.

Kathy was a funny and rational girl. Just like me, she also decided to go to China because of her painful relationships. After a few weeks, we started to share a lot and delved into more-in-depth discussions. Kathy was changing quickly, maybe too fast. In front of my eyes, she turned into an eager devotee for spiritual knowledge. We had endless conversations about the meaning of life, souls, and love. Soon we spend most of our time together, and my inner alarm was silenced by my wish to find a kindred spirit in China. That was a mistake I often made. My desire to see in others something that was not there had caused me some painful lessons.

The winter was slowly creeping in December, which meant not much sun and occasional rain. Although winters were much warmer than in Europe, there were no heaters in the houses, which made it more uncomfortable than the cold winters but warm interiors back home. One day, Kathy asked me to join her for lunch. She chose a Buddhist vegetarian restaurant, and she ordered her favorite fake Kung Pao chicken. I had vegetable noodles with divine blessings.

As soon as they brought our food, Kathy started, "I saw an interesting video about the power of the mind and the law of attraction." "What kind of video did you see?" I asked. Kathy went on providing me with a detailed description, and in the end, she added, "I had a realization after watching the video. What if I stayed positive all the time and did all these spiritual exercises and reach enlightenment?" Often it seemed that she wanted to become enlightened at all costs. Even more so since she was a perfectionist, always striving to be the best at everything. It was clear to me that this kind of motive had no chance for success because it is born out of the ego.

I paid attention to the particular way she looked when she spoke. In her eyes, I could see the ego trying to clutter her mind. Often when I speak with people, I can see their soul. It peeks out at me through their face, which becomes partially translucent and the features in their face change. There is always a white light sparkling with other light hues glowing in the face of the person. But sometimes, I can see the ego with its devilish flames in the eyes.

"I am not sure whether the primary focus should be on the enlightenment," I chose as a diplomatic answer. "As I understand it, the enlightenment means that the mind finds enlightenment, and we liberate ourselves of the bondage of our human self. The darkness is transmuted into light, and we can recognize the Truth instead of perceiving our old illusions. The mind restores its original function to see everything clearly, and we do not act out of painful emotional and mental bodies any longer. It happens naturally, without trying hard. The spiritual growth should feel natural as if it were the next logical step to take without forcing anything. If you feel that it is time to embark on a spiritual practice, let's say meditation, do it. But, do not force the right moment. Your heart and mind have to align first, and then enlightenment comes as a side effect.

Alignment is not about speed or quantity. It is not about having more but being exactly who you are - no more, no less. It is about aligning with your inner truth and acting on it. If your mind pushes your heart, then it causes stress and imbalance. This leads to much worse consequences than you or I can perceive. It is better to follow your intuition and be gentle with yourself on the spiritual journey," I said.

"But, you know, I do not understand why people are so stupid," Kathy continued. "They live like pigs, and they are blind. Average people do not see things clearly. I am not good with patience. I will make enlightenment happen," she exclaimed. "To me, it is just straightforward what to do, and I can see what people are doing wrong. It is as easy as that," Kathy finished. I hoped that she was only moody, and I let our conversation escape my mind as soon as we finished the food. Looking back, that was one of the bad omens I chose to ignore. Nowadays, I believe that the purpose of our meeting was to prepare me for my role as a spiritual teacher. I needed to understand how the ego plays its games and how it can darken someone's mind. That day, my desire to have a close friend won over doing what was right. Unfortunately, throughout our friendship, Kathy allowed me to witness how the ego's illusion of being special can control someone's behavior and how it tries to hurt others on purpose.

But besides Kathy, I also met many other friends. One of them was Tony, who was a Chinese language student at the local university. When I was looking for our flat, I could not speak Mandarin yet. Thus I went to check out a couple of flats with him because he was a fluent speaker. Not only did he help me to find an apartment for my classmates and me, but we also became good friends. Soon I introduced him to Kathy, and she fell for him immediately. It was a kind of teenage girl obsession. There was no space for rationality or patience.

The three of us began to meet frequently as we shared similar topics and ways of looking at the world. One evening we dove into in-depth topics, and it seemed that we all got along well. As the night continued, we went to a bar and discussed topics like Buddhism, Christianity, or energies. As the morning was approaching, Tony suggested that we go to Nanputuo. "You mean, like now?" Kathy wondered as it was shortly before five o'clock in the morning. "Yes, I mean right now," Tony replied. I knew he was serious, and I liked the idea, too. "Does anyone know what time they open the gate?" I asked. "They open at five in the morning. So, if we go now, we can see the sunrise from the summit," Tony said and stood to leave. "It has been decided then," Kathy smiled.

To reach the summit of Nanputuo temple, we needed to climb up a few hundred steps. Tony walked first, and I could see him walking with closed eyes, immersed in silent contemplation with his palms folded one above the other. I pointed to his hands to Kathy to indicate that we should stay silent and let him do his thing. I liked his mindful walk, and my thoughts slowed down too. The birds and nature were waking up to the new day as we arrived at the summit. We found a small rock to sit on and waited for the sunrise.

"Tony, what were you doing when we were walking up here?" I asked. "When I visited Japan, I stayed in a temple for a couple of months, and they taught me how to honor the energy of a temple with this walking meditation. At that time, when I came to Japan, I felt lost, and I was searching for answers about how to continue. First, I planned to stay for one month, but it turned into three months and then another six months in another temple, here, in China." "I have never met any westerner who has stayed in a temple," I was amazed. Since I was a little girl, I had often imagined that I would stay in a temple for a couple of months. The idea of being present and in silent service to the divine, combined with physical work, felt like a salve to my soul.

"What was the biggest teaching you found there? And did you find the inner peace that you were seeking?" "Oh," Tony sighed. "I still feel lost at times. Surely, less than before. I learned to meditate and exercise. Each day, we woke up at four o'clock in the morning to clean the yard, to help in the kitchen, and then to meditate. When this was done, we had a modest breakfast, followed by exercise. Then meditation again, food, some handwork, meditation, dinner, and evening prayers. Day in, day out. Such a routine definitely brings a sense of inner peace. It calms down the chattering mind. I felt great there. That is why I decided to come to the Chinese temple for even longer. In China, I stayed in a Shaolin temple, and we practiced martial arts every day. The monks told us that the martial arts cultivate the will and discipline. This was the first time in my life when I listened to myself. I had no idea that there was so much going on."

"That is fascinating. Tell us more," Kathy exclaimed. "I can show you pictures which I have from the Chinese temple. But, promise that you will not laugh." Tony said. "Haha. I cannot promise you that I will not laugh, but I want to see them anyway," Kathy winked at him. This was the first time I noticed Kathy flirting with him. I was happy that she met someone interesting to her. Perhaps Tony was the right guy for her.

Tony continued, "One day, I asked the chief monk, who counseled us, about my family. I asked him how I can feel grounded and self-confident, and he shared with me one

Japanese proverb. Although I would like to say it in the original, I am not sure if I can do it with my 101 Japanese language course," we both laughed together with him. "Yet if I dare to paraphrase it, it went like this, 'You were born of the Sun, here on Earth. The Earth is your divine mother, and the Sun is your divine father, the stars are your siblings. This is your origin. This is your only real family. You do not worry about anything. Just pray to the divine and recall your true origin," Tony said. We stayed chatting for a little more while gazing at sunrise over the sea horizon. It was a great way to welcome a new day.

CHAPTER 16

TWIN FLAMES

God split them into two.
Since eons, the two flames yearn to unite.
The seed of their love is forever pure,
Their hearts pound like the bright stars in the night.

The fire is too intense to keep them apart.
They mirror the soul in each other's eyes.
No secrets, no pretense, no lies,
Just the womb of the infinite night.

One feels the other one,
His thoughts,
Her wishes,
Their love.

What purity!
What sorrow!
Where did you go?
And where can I follow?

The snake woke up after eons of slumber.
Now, it slowly ascends the spine
Until our Light Bodies become brisker,
And we may reunite.

Things started to evolve quickly between Kathy and Tony.

Soon it became apparent that he did not feel the same way about her. However, at that point, Kathy had already made Tony special in her mind. I did not want to be the bearer of bad news, and some part of me hoped that I was wrong. When we were talking about him as we often did those days, I asked Kathy, "How does he feel about you? Are you going to see each other?" "Well, I am not sure when we see each other. But I think he must feel the same about me," Kathy replied. At that moment, my worries were confirmed because I knew that everything was happening mostly in Kathy's head.

It was a dilemma for me whether to tell her what I knew. On the one hand, she was my flatmate who became a friend, and I did not want to hurt her feelings and get too much involved with them. On the other hand, I knew Tony a little better. I did not think that he was looking for any commitments. From what I understood, she was not his type, and more importantly, I had found out recently that he was still in love with someone else. But what if my instincts were misleading me?

Did I have any right to take her hopes away? This was one of the reasons why female relationships were complicated for me. I am an honest and straightforward person, but I have also lost some female friends for my honesty. When what I had told them later showed up to be true, they would look for a culprit to ease their pain. As the prophet bringing unpleasant news, I was often found guilty for their misery. And it made me feel awful even though I knew that the ego likes to blame others for avoiding to take responsibility.

Still, it was hard seeing my best friends hating me because some guys did not feel the same about them. As if I could do something to change it. At that time, I still struggled to recognize when was the right moment to be quiet or to speak up. Speaking truth can also be the wrong choice when applied at the wrong time. How much could I intervene in someone's destiny? Was I supposed to say what I saw or let others get hurt? After all, it was about their lessons, not mine. When my friends asked me for insight, the answer was obvious, but if they did not, I eventually learned not to say anything.

After some contemplation, I decided to wait and see how things would unfold. From my own experience, I knew that when you are convinced that you love someone, then you overlook the red flags. I knew she would have gotten upset with me if I pointed out what she did not yet want to see.

Perhaps, I should have shared my opinion. If I could turn back the clock, I would certainly do it. Sometimes, it was easy for me to say things directly. Other times, it was tough when I knew that the other person would get upset. What was I afraid of? What made this case different from others? I decided to meditate on it as that was the simplest way for me to receive answers. Some moments later, clarity arrived.

Kathy was too close to me. She became like my family, and I was afraid to hurt her. Just like with my family, I would feel guilty for her possible unhappiness. I supported her illusion, and what was even worse, I acted against my gut feelings. Unintentionally, I created inequality between us. I placed her and her feelings above mine. I traded the truth for her acceptance. Yet, the reality was that I did not accept myself. I doubted myself in making the right decision. I allowed my past wounds to go against my inner integrity, which led to the strengthening of her illusions. I let our egos to form our friendship. My ego wanted to buy acceptance and love while her ego gained more space to protect the idea that Tony was special. So, I compromised my sense of integrity and truth and decided to stay quiet.

As I learned much later, this was a mistake. Unfortunately, as the following circumstances revealed, I was correct with my estimation of the situation between Kathy and Tony. Mostly, it was a one-sided affection, and Kathy had a challenging time to recognize it. She was not helped by the fact that she had misused some spiritual principles to help her achieve what she wanted. I started to receive more red flags about her behavior, and soon, I began to regret that I had ever taught her anything about spirituality.

This was one of the key lessons in my life because I had not been aware that someone eager for spiritual knowledge can misuse it. In my world of pure intentions, it had not crossed my mind that people may have personal motives for their behavior. Now I know that when someone opens up to spirituality, they initially experience new sensations and have eye-opening realizations. After some time, and the timing is highly individual, many people start to be influenced by lower entities and negative energies. This is part of the deal.

When we are new to spirituality, our ability to discern information is not yet refined. Lower entities want to take advantage of it, and they feed us wrong information here and there. If we ponder these twisted ideas, the entities know that they have hooked us up, and it is thus easier for them to slowly alter our perception. Around this time, people begin to have nightmares or sensations like a "higher" being communicates with them. This is a sensitive place to be as we are open to both positive and negative, and we need to choose only one of them as our master.

Some people get lost in this phase for some time. In some cases, they can even become crazy because entities can be extremely persuasive with their false messages. Like anything else in life, this is also conducted with our consent. At some level, mostly unconsciously, we give the green light to these entities by our interest in the twisted information they feed us. For many spiritual newbies, the hunger for knowledge outweighs their precautions about the source of information.

Lower entities cannot create anything new, they can only twist already existing creations. Therefore they always use something that we already believe to be true and then attach a false piece of information to it, only to confuse our minds. As I was open to spirituality since I was born, I went through these very unpleasant phases when I was young. Still deep inside, I knew that I was safe. I never turned away from God and love. As they have always been my guiding stars, these experiences have eventually passed.

Unfortunately, I did not recognize soon enough that this was happening with Kathy. Our relationship went up and down, depending on her moods. After some time, she began to attack me verbally and accusing me of things that were only occurring in her mind. Kathy accused me of not wishing her and Tony to be happy together. Naturally, this saddened me, not because of her words, but because I lost a friend. What I tried to avoid, happened anyway.

After a couple of months of studying in Belgium, we returned to China. At that point, my business studies were over, but since China supported my own inner growth so well, I knew since the first day that I needed to spend more time there. This time I decided to study the Chinese language at the same university in Xiamen. I once again decided to rent a flat with Kathy even though she often stopped talking to me for quite some time, and then she apologized and did the same again. I did not want to live with her as at that point, I could feel the dark energy around her, but somehow, I still hoped for things to turn out well. They did not.

After we returned to China, I decided to study a more advanced Chinese class than her. Since Kathy and I studied different levels of Mandarin, we did not see each other at school. While at home, she was locked in her room most of the time and did not speak to me much. I was not even sure whether she was still going regularly to school. I simply did not meet her anywhere – not at school and not even in our flat. Honestly, I did not mind because it was better that way. I did not have the energy for her mood swings.

Then, one day, she came to me unexpectedly and said to me like nothing had happened, "You should watch this video." "What is it about?" I asked. "I just watched it, and I think it is for you." Out of curiosity, I watched the video. The video was about soulmates and twin flames. I had not heard the term twin flames until that point.

After I saw it, Kathy explained, "You might have one or more soulmates. There is no guarantee of meeting them, but if you do, you grow a lot together because of your spiritual connection. Twin flames," she went on, "are quite different." We both remembered what Tony told us once, and Kathy repeated it that evening, "The God split one soul into two halves – into the male and female aspects, and since then they have been seeking each other."

Kathy then continued talking about what she had read; "Twin flame relationships evolve through many stages. When you first meet your twin, you feel an instant connection and a sense that you have found your home. After a while of meeting your twin flame, you have to be driven apart because you open up each other's wounds. All the fears, doubts, and negativity come to the surface. Their intensity overwhelms you. Because the connection with your twin is too intense, you must come apart. At this point, one of you may move to a different country or into another relationship. That is because one of you or both are terrified of the intensity of such a connection."

"You begin to run from each other, and during that time, each of you begins your own healing. Or should at least. This is to strengthen the connection to the divine. Once you heal yourself and your twin does the same, you are ready to reunite. There is a common mission for both twins. Your power together is unstoppable, so you have to get ready for the intensity, and then you can serve the whole world." After a short pause, she added, "There are seven stages, and they all fit you and Kahl."

I did not know what to think. Again, this was too personal for me to maintain a distance. She got me with the words "you and Kahl." These few words were ringing in my head during the whole night. "Why was she bringing up Kahl?" All I desired was to move on. For good.

CHAPTER 17

THE REVELATION

Somewhere over the rainbow
Lies the secret land.
In the earth of fantasies
Elephants carry them.

People lose their minds,
They trade their rights.
A fantasy shapeshifts into a reality
Creating distortions of all kinds.

Masses awaiting the revelation of the pink elephant,
They beg their gurus for a magic pill.
The reality is too heavy,
It can make you ill.

The flying rhinoceros is in the tree crown.
The golden goose is looking at him down.
From her cloud made of bright powder,
The whispers of people are getting louder.

How did you trade your knowledge?
For a slack patch?
Once you were on your path,
Now, it is full of dust!

The next morning, I decided to read more about the twin

flames, and the more I read, the more it seemed to be true. The stages of twin flame relationships related accurately to Kahl and me. It did make sense, and yet, it sounded lunatic. I was relieved to read how someone else described the magnitude of my feelings, but at the same time, an equally powerful inner unrest was building up within me. From my past, I knew that when something unsettles me, there is always some false information attached to it. I did not like the idea that I would be tight with Kahl forever because I did not see a way out of our situation. I still felt the intense connection and unconditional love for him, yet it was clear to me that we were not meant to be together. And these seemingly contradicting states of mind drove me crazy.

So I decided to go for a walk. I needed some space and time alone to regain my perspective and to redirect my thoughts on something else. When I got back home, I did more research and found someone online who claimed to be in a twin flame relationship. He was also guiding other twin flame couples and was counseling them. I liked the man because he was brutally honest in his videos, and he said that most people who believe that they had found their twin flames were wrong. They simply met their soulmates, and because it differed so much from their classical relationships, they felt that the description of twin flames applied to them.

This man said that only a tiny percentage of the population meet their twin flame in this lifetime. So, I hoped I belonged to that crazy majority who believed in twin flames but were wrong. He also said that the reunited twin flames have a sacred mission to serve the whole of humanity. They do not need to be famous, and they work on it energetically by creating new templates for every person on this planet. They are claimed to be the "strongest weapon" of the good forces as there is nothing more potent than the twin flame reunion and their love for each other.

For about a week, I considered contacting him. Eventually, I chose to see whether he could bring some clarity into my confused feelings. He replied quickly, and we had a session in two weeks. I was nervous as if he was about to deliver a death sentence. The confusion of my mind escalated. Before our Skype call, I was reading a lot about this topic and was astonished to learn how many people are talking about soulmates and twin flames. "What was going on? Why such an obsession? Does the labeling help anything?" I pondered.

The big day came, and I was ready online. After a short introduction, he said that he was about to call in his higher self to talk with me. "Thank you for the picture of the two of you that you had sent me," his higher self said. "I will explain to you what I am doing. With your kind permission, I am connecting to your system and reading your energies. I can also connect with your higher self. I think that you want to know most if you are in a twin flame connection, right?" He asked. "Yes, that is right," I reassured him.

"I will address your question directly. You have to understand that not many people experience the twin flame connection. This is not as common as it requires a certain maturity of the soul to handle the intensity. When I first saw the picture of the two of you, especially of yours and his eyes, I knew that this is a twin flame connection. Even without reading your energies, I recognized it instantly. Moreover, you are a potent and exceptional set of twin flames because you bring here to the planet unique energies that assist many people. Does this answer make you happy or not?"

"Actually, yes and no," I tried to process what he had

said. For me, it was more than yes or no answer. I did not know what that piece of information meant and what I was supposed to do with that. As though understanding the reason for our intense bond would change anything. After all, I was in it alone, without Kahl, and I sensed that I would always be. "I feel relieved, but I do not want to be with him. Actually, I am so scared to be with him," I continued. "Well, in fact, I expected such an answer," he said. "There are many fears related to your twin because you have a wounded self in you. As I read your energies, I see that you did not receive much love as a child. This made you think of yourself as someone who is less valuable than others. Your real fears originate from there, not from your twin. The connection is very intense and strong. Its strength also enhances the fears you both hold within you. In other words, there is too much light that makes the darkness to fight back even more. I can also read that Kahl has some energetic templates that reject a part of your energy. As long as he has it, he will not feel ready for you. It seems that this templating comes from his family." "That is how it feels to me as well," I confirmed his words.

"First, you have to focus on yourself. I can see that you have a huge awakened heart. Use this love to heal you. This is primarily for your own healing. When you heal the life will bring you back together. Yet you also have to know that some twin flames decide not to be together in this lifetime. This is a very bold decision because the yearning for each other will never dissipate. There is no guarantee that you will reunite even if you both got healed. Do you understand?" "Yes, I do," I answered. We continued talking more about the healing part than the twin flames, as I found it more relevant for me at that point in my life. I was surprised by the accuracy of his reading of my past and my energies as he continued talking about my childhood without knowing anything about me.

Coincidently, Kahl began to contact me again when I committed to my inner healing during the following couple of months. We exchanged calls or messages from time to time, and he expressed his hopes to see me soon. Kahl also told me that his girlfriend had left him. I thought that I had closed this chapter of my life, yet it came back through the back door once again. The time and distance did not seem to solve much.

For the following few months, I was thinking about the information that I had received. Most of the things this counselor said made sense. I was surprised to find out that many souls had similar experiences, and they perceived these counselors as gods. Whatever they told them must be true. Although this Skype session had helped me immensely, there was still something about this whole twin flame theory that did not feel right. Simply, I could not accept this theory wholeheartedly. I realized that I had to filter any messages through my heart and soul. We suppress our own inner wisdom and accept the thoughts of another person as reality. It can work as a harmful spell. We tend to think that what others say must be true. Yet what we often forget is that behind these powerful words, there are people just like us. They have an ego, too.

Some of the counselors perceive the world through their own filters if they do not tap into the higher consciousness before the session. In time, some gurus may become so convinced of their own righteousness that we start thinking that they must know better than we do. It is their firm conviction that makes their messages so appealing to masses. I understood that there are many levels of confusion in mind. Most of the spiritual teachers are healing themselves through their teachings. Teaching and learning are a mutual process, and a teacher also continues to be a student of life. Although healing yourself is a natural and harmless motive for starting to teach others, many begin before they are truly ready.

Although there is truth in what they teach, there is an attached illusion and misinformation as well because their minds are yet not healed. Thus the mind filters information through the dirty glasses. When the teacher is healed, his message is so powerful that it changes the lives of many – just as Jesus or Buddha were. They let go of the filters and chose to see the one and only truth. These teachers did not decide what would suit them. Instead, they decided to see what is real, which is – all is love.

As I was reading about the twin flame theories, I began to comprehend how dangerous it is to accept anyone's message without filtering it through your own guidance. First, we must be clear about who we are. Finding yourself is a long way, and we need to start from wherever we are. The stepping stones to healing may include having a teacher, reading books, and discussing with your peers, but never forgetting that we need to check whether a piece of information truly resonates with us. The best approach for me has always been to take what helps and let go of the rest. I ask my inner guidance, whether any bit of intelligence that I receive is in alignment with my inner truth. If not, I do not accept it no matter how appealing or widespread it may be.

It required some time to sort out the whole twin flame theory within me. What I came to believe is that some people made a soul contract before being born to awaken another person. When they meet, their spiritual heart awakens, and they receive the blessings to feel unconditional love. I believe that it is their new capacity to feel the unconditional love that makes them think that the other person must be their twin flame. The mind wants to justify and find a logical explanation for feeling unconditional love. Since the Source's love is beyond the limits of the rational mind, it finds the answer in special relationships. The essential purpose of the twin flame connection is anchoring unconditional love within this reality. That creates an energy grid around the Earth, which is charged with unconditional love. Does it matter what physical form, or not, the twin flame connection takes in this reality?

When we are confused, there are usually a few possible outcomes. One, we become crazy, and the ego takes over us entirely, and we perceive ourselves as special. We believe that we are better than others. Two, we begin to doubt spirituality and our inner guidance, so we detach from the whole spiritual world because it does not seem to work as we had hoped. Three, we learn to discern the information and hone our inherent ability to see the truth through the illusion.

Even though spiritual concepts are perfect for feeding twisted information, my experience with Kahl was simple. I met a man and immediately fell in love with him. The love was overwhelming. No matter what he did or did not do, the intensity of my love for him was stable, unlike the mind-based love when we get upset or blame others for our own emotions. This was not like anything I had known. After our meeting, I also started experiencing kundalini awakening and again began to have 5D visions and various spiritual experiences. And then, my inner growth skyrocketed once I decided to heal in China.

But never during that time did I believe that we would be together. They say that what you can imagine is possible for you. Well, I could not imagine us together. I was trying hard, but I could not, which was strange because my imagination is otherwise strong. This was my experience of the so-called twin flame connection. I chose to go beyond any theories, and as a result, I realized that I was a sovereign soul and that healing of myself is always the priority. Inner healing brings me closer to God, and it stands before anyone and anything else. My inner growth became my priority, and it magnetized me more than Kahl and all the theories combined.

Life is not about perfection - it is a process. And we are the active particles in this process. Even if it does not always look like it, we are the ones who determine the speed and intensity of our inner evolution. When we feel overwhelmed, our higher self stops sending us new insights and tasks to work on. Until we prove that we are mature enough to carry a more expanded vibration of light, we do not receive more. Thus we are indeed the ultimate referee. When we experience something truly difficult or unpleasant, our soul can fracture. We then withdraw our consciousness from various dimensions within our soul. It may be surprising that our mind can even block out specific memories when we encountered something too heavy to comprehend at that moment. We think that it did not happen even if it did. No matter what takes place in our life, at some level, we chose it.

So how is this all related to the concept of twin flames? I do not believe in a soul cut in two halves. At least from the perception of our 3D thinking, this concept is false. However, from the perspective of higher dimensions, it makes more sense. I am sorry, Plato, who first came up with this beautiful concept, but it got twisted along the way, and nowadays, it feeds the ego. In fact, I believe that such thinking is dangerous because it deprives us of claiming the sovereignty of our soul. We all have the ancient savior archetype stored up in our psyche. We believe that there is a savior out there. Perhaps in the skies. Perhaps in money. Perhaps in a special relationship. But all these concepts are built on lies.

According to my understanding, we were created as sovereign beings, and our capacity and potential are unimaginable. It often brings me to tears when I think of the human potential. For some reason, I can feel it and recognize it in others even though they cannot see it within themselves. I cannot possibly explain to others the power they carry within themselves because what I read in their hearts is so beautiful that the words fail me. Thus I do not think that we are mere halves of a soul. If we, the twin flames, work as a couple and we are wired the same way, then it is perfect. But if not, I do not think that we are screwed because we can work on our "missions" separately. When we meet our twin flame, we are ready to balance the feminine and masculine aspects within ourselves and create a direct link to the divine, so we have an opportunity to serve others in the most heart-centered manner possible. Whether we act on this possibility is entirely up to us. No pressure is needed because we have an unlimited amount of options to choose from when anchored on a higher level of consciousness within ourselves.

In my country, people are atheists, which does not mean that we do not believe in God. On the contrary, faith comes from our own experience; it is not taught. Thus everyone can find their own way to God, and no one judges the truth of others. No one tells us what we should believe. Although I do not know much about the world's religions, I believe in the universe, in love, God, Buddha, and also in Jesus.

Perhaps Jesus walked on this planet with his equal partner Mary Magdalene, and they were both expressions of healing and divine love for the masses. Perhaps Jesus and Mary Magdalene were closest to what Plato meant by the term twin flames. I believe that this is possible, but somewhere along the way, the truth got tangled.

From my experience and understanding, Jesus Christ brought unconditional love to this planet, and he energetically created a template of Christ's heart and consciousness. The energy template is available to us and has been ever since it was designed. When we are ready, Christ's heart is activated within us, and for it to happen, we do not need to be perfect to deserve it. When the time comes, it happens. Then we feel the unconditional love and our healing capacities and gifts are also increased. Thus perhaps your twin flame is someone who activates your Christ's heart, and this gradually leads to activation of Christ's consciousness. However, we do not need to meet our twin flame to activate it, it can also occur spontaneously or while listening to touching music or experiencing deep pain. Something that shakes our hearts.

Three years ago, I would not have believed that something like Christ's heart had existed, But all changed one night when I was sleeping in my parent's home. It was April, a month or so after I first met Kahl. My sister was sleeping in the same room with me as she often would when I came for a visit.

I slept soundly until something woke me up. My senses were immediately alert, and I was fully awake. I looked up above me, and there he was. I saw a colorful 5D Jesus Christ. His hair was moving as he was looking down at me. Apparently, I had nothing better to say in my initial shock than to exclaim, "Oh, Jesus!" It was a phrase that I would often use, but in this situation, it was very well applied. My voice was so loud that I wonder how come that my little sister did not wake up.

I do not know how long Jesus Christ was looking right into my eyes. It felt like ages, but probably it was about twenty seconds. The non-physical beings that I could see during nights were slightly transparent, but Jesus was not. I could see the color in his cheeks and hairs of his beard. He did not open his mouth to talk to me, but I received his messages telepathically.

Without a shadow of a doubt, I knew that he came to awaken Christ's heart within me. To paraphrase his telepathic message in my own words, it went like this, "Wake up! It is time! There is no time to hide anymore. Your time has come. You are here to heal the masses, and you know it." And then I also received the message that said something like: "What are you doing with your life? You know who you are. Now is the time to act accordingly. Stop running away from your true self and your work here on Earth. Why are you still hesitating?" Then he disappeared, and the room was covered in a ruby light that remained for a couple of minutes.

To make sure that the message got through, within the following week, I also saw Mother Mary with her heart shining brightly. Her message was the same. Nevertheless, I did not act on their guidance for at least the following year and a half. I was afraid of living up to their messages, although I knew that it was the time. I did not wish to walk this path alone, and in the beginning, I hoped that I could share it with Kahl. This hope that was not supported by my belief kept me stuck from following my life calling.

Before these experiences, I doubted when someone saw Mother Mary or Jesus Christ. I thought that it was quite unlikely until I experienced the same. Now I know this is not just possible, but the Christ consciousness is available for everyone. He is continually guiding us. Maybe now it is more significant than ever. And I also understood that my encounter with Kahl was related to it. Kahl was my wake-up call.

CHAPTER 18

THE ROCK CLIFF VISION

As the star shines its light,
I have seen you in me.
You are my dark knight.
Please, do hold me tight.

I have never heard your voice so strongly.
Now, I feel the beat of your heart.
Please, love me gently,
And never come apart.

Be the magic in my life,
Be the crystal that cures my heart.
For the wisdom let me thrive,
Or sorrow slowly kills me.

Where is your temple?
Where is your shrine?
You, the knight of sorrow!
You, the herald of woe!

Come closer to me,
So I can hear your whispers.
We share the language of the stars,
The places beyond our lives.

You are my body.
You are my soul.

I have seen you in me
As the darkest cloud.

It was a cold Saturday, and I was working on a paper for one class. I was warming myself up with a cup of tea when suddenly, something extraordinary happened. I could feel intense alien energy entering me. My whole body started to shake, and so I decided to breathe deeply and wait for it to pass. However, the energy did not want to leave. Instead, its vigor made me accept it.

As I embraced the energy, I received a vision that played out in front of me as if I were part of a movie. I witnessed myself standing on a rock cliff and staring at a vast ocean. It was a late sunny afternoon, and I was soaking into an endless space in front of me. I felt my heartbeat, the flapping wings of seagulls, and the smell of roses. With every breath, I was enjoying the pure existence. As I was savoring the beauty around me, someone put his hand on my chest. My heart began to pound faster, and adrenaline got released into my veins and arteries. My pupils widened. I was paralyzed and unable to turn around to see who was standing behind me, but I knew this hand. It belonged to Kahl.

In the same nanosecond, as Kahl touched my chest, the sun kissed the horizon. Our eyes intersected with the center of the sun. The timing had to be perfect. All at once, the sky opened to unravel its secrets to us and time accelerated. We entered a different space-time reality. The heavenly bodies descended from the womb of the space, and we watched galaxies, solar systems, and planets. As we traveled the space-time, we entered one galaxy and solar system after another when the movement began to slow down. Two suns appeared in front of us, and then we saw it - a beautiful world adorned with high mountains, unusually tall trees, and vast oceans.

We could see a white domed building with three smaller cupolas. We entered the building by penetrating its organic walls, and then we landed in the heart of the building. When I looked around, I could see twelve beings that were sitting in a circle around us. Kahl and I looked at each other in confusion. Yet none of the beings around us seemed surprised. As if they were waiting for this encounter for a long time. "Welcome back, Lavinia," the beings said in unison without opening their mouths. "You have been highly expected. The vibration lines intersected at the right moment; thus, the portals opened." The beings continued communicating telepathically with us. "We have missed you dearly. You have stayed on Terra longer than it was foretold."

Suddenly one of the beings came to me and grasped my head, and with an urging look, he told me, "Lavinia, you have to start remembering who you are. It is time to wake up. You cannot save him. Come back home. You are both reminding each other the original frequency of your soul's power, and you bring it to people on Terra. The frequency is awakening within both of you. I will be in continuous contact with you. Do not worry. Things will come together soon."

A second later, Kahl and I were pulled back into our bodies on Earth. Back to the rocky cliff.

Although my body was shivering, everything soon returned to normal, and my heartbeat slowed down. Although this vision was so unusual compared to the ones that I was used to having, I knew deep within that Lavinia and Kahl were our real names somewhere in the stars.

CHAPTER 19

THE POWER OF DETACHMENT

Two masters are pulling you apart.
Whom shall you serve?
Whom shall you part?
Beware, so you get the destiny you deserve.

The voice of love,
the cry of fear,
Both standing in front of you.
Whom shall you believe?

The night has not come yet,
Return safely back.
Follow my voice
Into blissful joy.

My relationship with Kathy went through many motions and phases. One of our common friends once told me that she was extremely jealous and envious of me. The friend said that Kathy did not wish me any good and that she was competing with me the whole time. After learning the news, I was shocked at first, but then it all made sense. All her ups and downs.

One Friday afternoon, when I returned home from my classes, Kathy was waiting for me. At that point, we did not speak with each other anymore. Without any warning, she shouted at me, "I hate you. I really hate you and wish you all the worst in the world. I want you to die." I stood there like hot water had scalded me. There was no thought whatsoever in my mind. I had no clue why Kathy had said it, but I knew that I did not want to react. I did not want to be a part of her problems anymore.

Instead of reacting, I quietly prayed, "Soul, please, show me how I should respond." Then it hit me, "Send her love." So I did. Kathy was still looking at me with her hateful piercing eyes and a reddish face. But I chose to remain neutral and said, "Okay, Kathy. You have a right to feel whatever you feel. I still love you." Then I stood in front of her in complete silence. An absolute peace took over me.

She looked at me baffled and said, "You do not get it or what? I hate you!" So I repeated with a calm voice, "It is okay, Kathy. I love you." She looked at me for a few more seconds and then disappeared into her room. I went to my room and started to paint a picture while listening to some piano music. I felt peaceful and relieved. I directed all my focus on the present moment.

Knock. Knock. I heard. "Can I talk to you?" I heard Kathy saying. Although I was surprised, I still felt perfectly calm, so I opened the door. "I am sorry for what I said. I do not know what got into me. Can you forgive me?" She apologized. "It is fine. There is nothing to forgive," And I meant it.

There was nothing to forgive because her words had no power to touch me. This amazing experience taught me to understand the power of love. Although Kathy was furious, one genuine sentence flipped the situation for both of us. This experience helped me to realize that I am free and do not need to react to anything. It gave me the freedom to choose not to play a part in someone else's ego illusions.

To this day, I cannot say what was going on deep within

her. I think that she was trying to find herself, too. I also knew how the intensity of certain illusions could shatter one's thinking. All that was more than understandable, and I felt compassion for her. But since she did not gain control over her jealousy and envy, there was nothing to solve. I decided to cut-off our relationship and focus on myself. And Kathy chose to spend most of the time with her new boyfriend, which was very good for both of us. It allowed us more space.

So my new chapter in my Chinese adventures began.

CHAPTER 20

INNER HEALING

A beautiful little girl is sitting in a corner,
Dressed in black leaky armor,
Weeping so pitifully that even the crows woke up
To look at the poor thing disrupting their sleep.

The crows landed slowly
To see her stained face from the ashes
And her wind-swept golden hair,
Her tears caught up in the lashes.

At that moment, the angry crows whose sleep was
disrupted
Transformed into the white swans whose hearts melted.
Terrifying screams turned into a graceful voice,
No more of the ugly noise.

The swans took up her little arms,
Lifted them in the air a couple of times.
Their white feathers turned into a white robe,
Its grace and glamor covered the globe.

Now, the charming highest priestess
Opens up to the vastness,
To the new life emerging in front of her,
Her inner queendom shinning with divine brightness.

Once I closed the chapter with Kathy for good, I had more capacity to dive deeper into my healing. I knew that there was one thing I could do more – to apply spiritual knowledge in my daily life. It was not enough to read esoteric books or to meditate. One thing is to grasp and comprehend complex concepts intellectually. Yet it is an entirely different universe to act on that information. I hesitated to take action out of fear. For a long time, I had been accustomed to living in emotional pain, so it had not come to me overnight to change it. Not even after meeting Kahl. Healing my wounds was something I needed to do. Strangely, I was not afraid that I would not know how to do it. But I was scared of what the healing would mean for my future life.

Living abroad offers a fresh perspective on life. It provides a distance and detachment from the familiar. When you are alone, you start to think for yourself, and the rumors of the known world slowly quieten. Living in a new country for a limited period teaches you to cherish your time. Only the present moment exists. At least this is how it was for me. Knowing that these exciting days would eventually come to an end taught me to value what life gifted me much more. All the gorgeous people I met, the places I visited, and the traditions that I got a chance to explore became my teachers.

Each person and every place taught me some lessons. There were distinctive kinds of blessings in every encounter. Most of them were positive, some were harder, but all of them were worth it. Everything opened my soul a tiny bit more. My heightened senses were aware of each fleeting moment. Now that the last bit was ahead, I wanted to face it with all it had. I was soaking up the life itself and brought spirituality into everything I did.

One of the beneficial habits that I learned in China was to apply the Chinese saying, "go sleep early, get up early." Without much effort, I developed morning and evening routines that carried me throughout the last months. I began to get up earlier to have time to meditate and do sports before I needed to catch the bus to school at seven o'clock. I was surprised when I ran out of the flat after meditation at 5:30 in the morning and saw how many older people were already practicing Tai Qi in the parks along the sea path where I liked to run.

Together with new routines, devoting even more time to my inner healing felt natural. Healing myself felt like remembering; I knew precisely what to do. The techniques were coming to me intuitively, and I acted on them without hesitation. I was releasing one old story that used to define me after another. Gradually I was coming closer to the true me buried under the layers of my past.

I realized that some problems did not belong to me; instead, I had picked them up from others. This is something that empaths do unconsciously. Unknowingly, I took on the problems of others because of my willingness to help them. How better do you help someone than taking on their burdens? However, since I was not aware of what I had always been doing, other people's dense energies felt like my own. After all, I experienced them in my body, so they must have been mine, I assumed.

But as my ability to read energies improved, I could recognize which energies did not belong to me and could sense whose they were. As I started clearing out my energy body that harbors our energies and emotions, I became happier and freer. Finally, I could feel my true self, the self that was unaffected by other people's emotions, beliefs, thoughts, and energies. I recognized my soul's blueprint -

my true essence. It brought me such joy that I could not stop laughing. My aura of happiness became contagious, and people reflected it to me in kind smiles and little acts of unexpected favors.

Feeling and experiencing my soul's essence was mending my heart and my old wounds. I stopped needing things on the outside because I was becoming whole inside. Although I still had challenges, they did not throw me off the course as much as they used to do. Before my transformation, I would spend weeks or even months feeling sad because of something from my past. But after clearing out my energy body, I could create a distance between myself and situations. Finally, outer circumstances were losing their grip on me.

During weekends when I had more time, I was painting or writing in the mornings. I also bought myself a keyboard, so I could continue playing the piano. Almost every evening, I went alone for long walks into the hills near my place. Sometimes I would set off after sunset. It was refreshing to meditate in the forest in the dark. Up in the hills was my secret spot, a huge, rather flat rock where I would study, read or meditate. The rock offered me a beautiful view over the opposite hills, valleys with trees, and to the sea in the distance. I spent hours there. Most of my realizations and healings happened in this magical spot. Where else than in the woods again.

CHAPTER 21

GREG

The feathers of Angels were falling from the skies,
They rushed down my cheeks like velvet silk.
The divine signs flow to us at all times,
In the realms of heaven, there is no split.

Before we entered this world, I held your hand.
Together we vowed to enhance our evolution.
Now we march alongside on the vast land,
Ready to stir up each other's soul revolution.

Do you remember my breath flowing gently on your neck?
Before we were born, you promised to recognize the
rhythm of my heart,
To draw in the Breath of Remembering as an ancient
Melchizedek,
You swore to hold the torch of Light and let it forever
impart.

Each encounter is an echo of these sacred pledges.
The sparkles in our eyes remind us of who we are
Before they turn into pale ashes
To bring us the forever dust of the stars.

The series of little coincidences that let me to Greg was
astounding. After all, I was always introduced to my
partners through a series of accidents. And it always

reminded me how we could not plan for the critical turning points in our lives. They happen without our interference. With Greg, it was no different. Soon, I found out that the universe had another surprise in stock for me – to heal my wounded heart.

About halfway into my Chinese studies, I decided to spend two nights a week on the campus. I had a room for free in the dorms since the beginning, but I did not use it because I preferred to stay closer to where I lived the previous year. In addition to that, living outside of the campus offered me numerous daily chances to practice my Mandarin with locals. Nevertheless, after a couple of months, I decided to stay in the dorms to focus solely on my studies. Next to the dorms was a newly built spacious swimming hall, which was mostly almost empty. I was going there for long swims after my classes, and once a week, I went with three of my friends to visit an organic farm next to the campus to support the old couple who ran it.

One evening, I was in my room exercising yoga when the doors were pushed open. An Australian girl was standing at the doorstep, and she claimed that it was her room. She was entirely convinced about it, and she seemed to be similarly shocked as me. I was astonished because I could not understand why she believed my room to be hers. Rightly, in her mind, she wanted me to leave, and the conversation was getting a bit heated from her side.

Then I asked her to calm down and take a look around so she could notice that there were my things in the room. When she glanced around, she felt embarrassed by the sudden realization that it was indeed my room. Immediately, she began to apologize, and we both laughed sheepishly. Her room was one floor above mine, and as she was hurrying back home, she did not realize that she missed one floor. The whole situation was slightly awkward, and we exchanged a few polite sentences to steam out the weirdness. We were probably unsuccessful, though. I kept seeing her here and there, and each time we exchanged greetings and continued with our own business. For me, the whole situation was fairly amusing, but I could read the embarrassment in her eyes each time I run into her.

Once, before the winter break, I was returning from the swimming pool late in the evening, and I run into her at the stairs. She was chatting with another girl whom I had not met yet. I greeted her and overheard a piece of their conversation about a trip to Thailand. I also planned to visit Thailand during the upcoming one-month break, so I decided to ask them for more details about their plans. The other girl, Lara, happened to look for someone who would accompany her to Thailand. She seemed nice, so we exchanged our phone numbers.

After swapping a few messages with Lara, we agreed to go to Thailand together. How easy it is to arrange these things when you are a student in a foreign country! One afternoon, we met at a coffee shop to buy our flight tickets. While we were searching online, Lara admitted to me that she did not have the budget for it. She apologized and said that, unfortunately, she was not coming with me. I understood her situation as I also often had too little money to pursue my dreams. Yet that time, I had been saving up money from random jobs, so I was determined to go. I did not know whether I would ever come back to Asia again, so I wanted to make the best out of it.

I booked my flight tickets, and after we had talked for a little longer, Lara said that she was going to attend a lecture later that night. A friend of hers was organizing lectures on different topics, and the speakers were expats living in China. That night, the lecturer was a representative of a chain of renowned five-star hotels in China. I decided to join her, and we left the coffee shop and headed to the hipster area of Xiamen.

"You have to take off your clothes if you want to come in," a smiley Russian man told me as I was standing at the entrance. "I do not think so," I replied and walked into the room. He was resilient for a couple of minutes, but then I managed to disappear off his sight. "That was Greg," Lara said. "He is the organizer, and as you figured out, he likes to play jokes." "Yes, I can see," I laughed.

Such remarks did not take me out of balance. A long time ago, I figured that the best way to stop those silly comments is ignorance. If that does not work, then a rough look right into their eyes would do. Although these men are annoying, they are mostly harmless. Some men probably perceive themselves as kings of the jungle. While many others do not know how to approach women directly, and they attempt to hide their insecurities behind similar masculine phrases.

Before the lecture started, I introduced myself to a Chinese lady who happened to own a Chinese language school. I was playing with the idea of taking some extra classes outside the university so that I would have more chances to focus on what I needed. As I was speaking with her, some other people said that they were studying at her school and they were satisfied with the teachers. So I considered taking one extra class a week in her school to practice my spoken Chinese. As we dove into a conversation with the Chinese lady, I also mentioned my trip to Thailand and Cambodia, but I assured her that as soon as I was back, I would start. Greg overheard our conversation and exclaimed in his masculine voice,

"Thailand! I also want to go there! Let's go together!" I was laughing and thinking, "Yes, sure, we will go together. I have never met you before, and you told me to take off my clothes as the first thing. I would be stupid to go with you."

At the end of the lecture, Greg invited me to join him and two other people for dinner. After some persuasion, I joined them. We spent a couple of hours in the restaurant, and then I left with Greg in a taxi. Coincidently we happened to live near to each other. Not sure why, but I gave him my phone number after he insisted. Perhaps because earlier at the bar, I could see that he had a kind heart and was extremely funny. I have always had a weakness for men who can make me smile. As I was leaving the taxi, he kissed me on my lips instead of cheeks and reassured me that he was coming to Thailand with me.

When I recall how many little coincidences let to our meeting, I must smile at the ways the universe orchestrates things. When we get out of our minds and go with the flow, we allow the universe to support us on our inner healing journeys. If the Australian girl were not sure that my room was hers, I would not have met Lara. If Lara were not convinced that she wanted to join me in Thailand, I would not go for that lecture. Moreover, if she had not changed her mind, nothing that was to follow next to open my heart even further would not have happened.

CHAPTER 22

ENERGY BLOCKAGES

You came to initiate my soul,
To help me embark on a new role
Through the dark nights and grief.
Our times together were too brief.

You were masked as a tormentor.
My heart set off on a cruiser,
While you were caught up in daily motions,
Getting lost in the vast oceans.

I confused your help with love,
While you only gave me a shy blush.
I wished you would usher in your fondness,
Instead, you brought me a verdict of coolness.

Our companions are our greatest teachers.
Often, they turn into preachers.
You covered your words with cynicism,
Immersed in your pessimism.

What could have been love,
Turned to lust.
Now, nothingness is in your heart,
Love only in the head can never start.

It is a curious phenomenon that sometimes when we are allowed to relax after a long while, we first get sick. Instead of enjoying a well-deserved peace, the suppressed emotions come forth, and our body breaks down. Although I was not ill, my body was still shaking after realizing the full extent of the suppressed stress I had been feeling. It all surfaced during the winter break. My stress levels were extremely high, yet for years, I had not acknowledged it because there was no safe space to face the stress I was dealing with.

I went to my favorite spot and sat down on the rocky cliff. As I was admiring the birds playing in the air, I recalled the last summer when I went to visit a kinesiologist my friend had recommended to me. The kinesiologist could tell many things about me and my life based on the pressure in my arms. Her findings were remarkably correct, and it was a piece of cake for her to read situations from my childhood. She also measured my stress levels. Then she looked at me with a surprise in her eyes, and she informed me that my stress levels were ten times higher than the usual maximum. She compassionately told me that most people would lie unconscious in a hospital with my stress levels. Back then, I assumed that it could not be true, but during my inner healing journey, lastly, I noticed how much stress I had been concealing.

When I still lived with my family, there was constant pressure in the air and one problem after another. I was continually shaking inside, waiting for another catastrophe to come. I was slowly trained to believe that life was a struggle and that problems would always arise. Whenever I had a moment of peace, I knew that some terrible issue was just behind the corner. And guess what? Something new always came up.

I saw the kinesiologist twice in total. The second time, she helped me understand even better the connection between my upbringing and current life. As an unplanned side effect, I realized how my faulty perceptions had kept me from being with Kahl. When I met Kahl, I did not believe I could experience true love. Although nowadays I like to think that both of my parents loved me, they were unable to show it. Then my teenage crushes on the wrong guys did not help me to shape a healthier self-image. Above that, my inability to leave Luke earlier undermined my confidence. Everything led me to believe that I cannot accept love because it was dangerous. I could feel the inner resistance to receive love. And with Kahl, I wanted him to love me, but I never let him close. Neither did he.

But now I was alone, and for the first time, I felt safe and protected. The protection did not come from an external source; it sprang from within me. I felt my soul wrapping me in a soft silk blanket and assuring me that everything would be fine. And I trusted. I had never felt such safety and peace as in the arms of my soul. Thus I committed myself to allow any suppressed feelings to come to the surface.

Intuitively I started to care about my home environment for the first time. I had not felt cozy at home for ages. Taking care of my immediate surroundings was new to me. The desire to have a clean, light, and pleasant environment came from within me. I craved to turn my home into a beautiful sanctuary, but in my previous relationship, it had not been possible as this desire was not shared. Besides, we were frequently moving with my ex-boyfriend. This time I decided to start right there where I was, although I knew that my days in China would come to an end. Nothing could stop me anymore from creating a light and vibrant home. First, I used watercolors to paint a couple of pictures and hung them on the walls. I bought myself a lovely quilt, flowers, and candles. Thus each time I returned home, I felt welcomed and good. My environment became highly inspiring to me, and it provided me with a perfect shelter for my renewed period of healing.

While reorganizing my flat, I also allowed long-accumulated feelings of anger, grief, sadness, and a sense of hopelessness surface so that I could finally acknowledge them. My primary goal for addressing my emotions was to find inner peace. As I was working with my suppressed emotions and stress that had been piling up for decades, I noticed that creating stories to explain why something had happened would only lead me deeper into the victimhood. To release old traumas and wounds, we need to comprehend their lessons. The purpose of revisiting the past is not to delve into excuses and victim mentality, but to move on with expanded knowledge. At the very beginning of the energy work that helped me move past my old wounds, I realized that emotions are harmless and neutral. The pain is caused by the stories that we invent to support our feelings. Since we unconsciously kept ourselves from feeling the full spectrum of our emotions in challenging moments, those suppressed emotions then move to our subconscious mind. Consequently, they form the stories about who we are and what we should do to prevent additional pain.

The reality and circumstances always catch us at our weakest spot. This is the way of life to help us heal. Everything that we suppress and deny keeps returning, until one day, we acknowledge it and release it for good. I needed to get rid of was the story that I was a victim of my past. Unconsciously, I was pushing people away from me so I would protect myself from any potential pain. I was utterly confident that everyone wanted to hurt me and that I could not trust anyone. Then after I had managed to push them away, my ego took it as the evidence that no one loved me.

A curious thing that happened when I paid attention to the twin flame theory was that I began to separate myself from others. My ego was creating a bubble around me. Subconsciously, I believed that no one could comprehend what I was experiencing, and no one I knew seemed to have experienced the kind I had with Kahl. With him, it was far from a typical love crush. Even if I did not accept the twin flame theory entirely, still on a deeper level, I was detaching from others who could not understand it. It put me into a vacuum where all I could hear were the reverberation of my own incessant thoughts.

Later, I learned that the ego wants us to feel separated from each other. It loves to raise walls between us so that we can feel lonely and isolated. Undoubtedly, I could feel the invisible wall before I met Greg. However, it did not feel right, and I did not want to live in a world of separation. Even though I felt love for everyone and everything, even in this space and my heart was wide open, it was just a one-way stream. I did not allow others to reach me in my bubble. It needed to crack.

CHAPTER 23

UNLOCKING MY HEART

Pieces of broken crystals crushed my heart,
A million fragments made every motion hurt.
What could have been heaven is now apart,
The land of shining diamonds turned to a speck of dirt.

Every pain made my commitment to love stronger.
No one else is the judge of my life.
The magic happens when I pull the fragments closer,
Within my heart shall be no more strife.

I wait no longer for you to come.
In the biggest abyss, I found myself.
Now I hear the beat of the drum.
No one near me, not even yourself.

My heart cracked wide open.
This time it shall stay.
The spirit of unconditional love woken
Into a brand new exciting day.

A day before the Chinese New Year, I set off west to
Guangzhou, where I stayed with my friend, whom I met
last year in Xiamen. I spent two lovely days with him. We
were visiting old temples, met his friends in the evening,
and we strolled in the parks before I left for Thailand. As
always, I traveled light and without plans. Luckily, right

after my arrival at the airport in Thailand, I met an old couple who offered me to share a taxi with me, and they quickly instructed me on everything related to Thailand. They turned out to be almost locals as they had spent every winter in Thailand for the last decade.

First two days, I rested at the beach. For the first time after a long while, I had a proper beach holiday. It was late afternoon, and I was reading a book when my mobile unexpectedly beeped. "Hi Sylvia, I just arrived in Phuket. I will rent a motorbike, and then I will pick you up tomorrow. Where are you staying? Greg." I was staring at the screen speechless. Over the last couple of days, I had forgotten entirely about Greg's assurance to join me. Besides, we did not agree on any specifics and had not even been in contact lately. Thus, I had concluded that his intention to join me was not serious. His message took me by a sheer surprise. I hesitated for quite a while before I replied. "Hi Greg, I am in Kata beach." The reply came swiftly, "Great! I will pick you up tomorrow at 9 am." I tried to focus on reading after we had exchanged a few more messages, but my mind was full of wonder about his behavior. He did not seem to worry about anything and always did what he wanted.

The morning came soon. I got up at five o'clock and went to a coffee shop across the road to have some light breakfast and to write a few articles before the streets got busy. It was my holiday morning ritual, observing sunrise while sipping coconut water and pouring my heart on pages for the readers of my first website. At these early hours, no one else was there except my happy mood and a tide of creative ideas relentlessly flowing onto pages.

The early morning hours flew by, and nine o'clock approached. Just as Greg had promised, he and his broad smile arrived on a motorbike. First, we went for another breakfast, and then we hit the road and drove north to explore Phuket. We often stopped on the way to capture the beauty of our surroundings. Taking photos turned out to be our shared passion, except that I have never shared mine with anyone afterward. I have traveled to many countries and could have become a travel blogger easily. Practically none of my friends ever knew which countries I have visited because I never talked about it unless someone asked me for travel tips. I enjoyed exploring the shore and savored the air in my hair. I had sat on a motorbike only once before, but that day with Greg, I fell in love with the freedom and spontaneity it offered. Our journey took us to a perfect beach, Bangtao, which back then was still pristine. The white sandy beach spreads for a couple of kilometers, yet it was not full of tourists and vendors back then when I was in Phuket for the first time. We walked for quite a bit, and then we found a spot to lie down.

Our conversation flowed in a relaxed manner, and we were laughing the whole time. However, I could not stop wondering what Greg wanted from me. Why did he come? If I had learned one thing, then it was to be cautious with men. After my broken heart with Kahl, I did not have any thoughts of getting myself into another relationship. I had also begun to distrust men's intentions. No matter how sweet their words were, it did not reach me through the thick walls I had built around my heart. I had grown skeptical about the matters of romantic love.

My heart was lovingly open to old grannies in the streets. I loved every bit of nature and was an admirer of its beauty. I cherished the life of animals, and they were always happy to approach me without fear as if they could sense my love. I adored my friends, and I was sending blessings to my family. But, at that point in my life, I was not able to receive love other than from spirit and nature. In my mind, I was done with human love that had given me many sleepless nights and restless days.

As the universe would have it, I found myself at a beach with the man who did not seem to care about the walls around my heart. We had an easy-going discussion, and I felt carefree until I noticed that maybe his interest in me was not solely as a friend. This set my alarms on, and I used all my tactics to make someone leave. But nothing worked with Mr. Greg. He was a child of fortune and did not suffer from negative thoughts and fears.

I soon learned to adore Greg, for he seemed to live in sweet oblivion where everything was positive and had a solution. To my surprise, he had not read many spiritual books, yet he was living by some of the fundamental principles that I and many others were trying to embody the hard way. Greg was a master of being in the present moment. There was not a single worry that he could not dissipate with a blink of an eye. His character was kind and welcoming. I struggled with him for a couple of days, but soon, it became clear to me that the walls of my heart would not stand his presence. My heart began to melt and open up to his love, warmth, and immediacy.

Somewhere there by the Andaman Sea, the walls around my heart faded away, and I remained vulnerable ever since. The universe had to send me a master opener of women's hearts. Taking down these thick walls is one of Greg's many gifts. He could not have failed, not even with me. We became very close. With him, I became more rooted in the present moment, as well. Nothing else was possible. This is how his presence works magic with others.

During the holiday, we spent many beautiful moments talking until late hours. Greg is a man with heaps of love.

Not just for me but for everyone. His heart is like a diamond shining to his environment, and anyone who is drawn near him is bound to fall victim to his childlike love and spontaneity. When our days together were approaching the end, we took a boat trip to the surrounding islands, Phi Phi, and some other islands which names I never remembered. Greg's close friend joined us too, and we enjoyed a lovely day filled with diving. Early the next morning, I continued alone in Bangkok.

I had a few days in Bangkok, which allowed me enough time to explore the city on my own. I love to stroll in the streets and let my legs lead me. When I travel, I can walk the whole days from sunrise to sunset without getting tired. I need to connect with each place at my own pace. When I close my eyes, I can see flashes of what has happened in those places. Each location whispers me its own story.

But the most, I felt attracted to 'wats,' the Buddhist temples in Bangkok. I set off on a boat early in the morning so that I would not need to hurry while exploring these gems of history. Although the temple area was overcrowded with tourists, somehow miraculously, I would always find spots where I was entirely alone and could immerse myself in deep meditation. Whenever I could, I would sit on the floor, raise my palms facing outward and move my fingers gently. My upper torso would then start moving by itself in the rhythm of the frequencies around me. As the energy moved my body, I could read the energetic patterns of the wats and unite with their vibration.

In this way, I can feel the frequencies of any place. All I need is solitude and time to connect with the area. Often the frequencies flow into my throat, and I begin to sing in unknown languages. Each place has its own unique song, and each word is an echo of ancient times. Every person who has ever lived leaves here an energetic signature, and as those energy threads flowing from every individual intertwine with each another, they create an unparalleled tapestry of energy that contains valuable knowledge. Already as a little girl, I could translate those energies into words and feelings.

When I reached a fountain in the temple complex, I was overflowing with love. The sunset was slowly kissing the top of the temples and shimmering in my hair. I pulled out my journal and began to capture the blessings I had received that day. It was one of those moments of clarity when I could see my future. Suddenly, I knew that everything would turn out well. I could see that my love for others can ignite their hearts and help them to tap into their own magnitude. For me, the fact that we are all equal at the soul level is not a concept; it is something that I feel and understand in every cell of my body. That day stayed in my memory as an oasis of peace and reconnecting with the universe. Something precious was born within me.

After strolling around the wats, I still had a couple of days to explore other areas and meet a friend with whom I studied business last year. He moved back to his hometown, Bangkok. On my last day, he drove me to the airport, and I was ready for the final leg of my travel in Angkor Wat, Cambodia.

CHAPTER 24

MEDITATION WITH THE KHMERS

An immemorial remembrance overfloods my body,
Spreading through the veins of eternal life.
What once was buried is no longer cloudy,
The prophecies long forgotten ran rife.

A ruby rose descended from the heavens
Floating into the heart of the priestess.
Her diamond crown forthwith brightens,
Her spirit flies open, and energy widens.

Fluttering wings of dragonfly bear the golden dust,
Dispelling it in the air molecules,
Forming all around me an enchanted gust,
Overflowing with radiant jewels.

The time has come to remember my origin.
The mists of forgetfulness are now lifted.
Out of the ashes of the old world poured into the resin,
There stands a priestess who is heavenly gifted.

The veil between the ages now slackens,
The trunk of the ancient tree reveals its secret.
The twinkle on the lake brightens,
Offering me the wisdom to keep it.

My brief visit to Angkor Wat, Cambodia, did not start well.

After processing the visa at the airport, I found out that someone had mistakenly taken my backpack instead of theirs. Our bags were identical, but I immediately noticed that the backpack left in the baggage claim was not mine because it had a violet scarf wrapped around it. When I went to airport security to report what happened, I was disappointed to see that they did not seem to care about it. So I had to pull out my stubborn side, and I sat down and told them that I was not going to leave until they had found my backpack. To motivate them even further, I started talking nonstop because I know it can drive some people crazy. When I am in the mood, I can speak incessantly, and I am often in such spirits. It is one of the attributes that can help me in similar situations to get lazy people to work. As by a miracle, I got my backpack in two hours.

I also called my hostel to inform them that I would check-in later, and they sent me a rickshaw driver to pick me up. On the way, I agreed to have him for the next two days to drive me around the temples. Immediately, I connected with the driver, who seemed to be a kind man trying to earn an extra few dollars from tourists to provide food for his big family. This was the part of human lives that had always been the most challenging for me to witness. In the west, most people worry about superficial things. Here, a few thousand kilometers east, people feel blessed to earn a few dollars a day to feed the whole family.

One of the poorest places that I had seen was the Philippines. People did not even have floors in their homes. They only had stomped soil beneath their feet and palm leaves above their heads. That was it. I also saw many young male prostitutes on the edges of the roads, which until that point, I never knew that even existed. Later I learned that also Filipino women need to offer themselves online to find wealthier western husbands. And to my surprise, it works. The deals are made, and I wonder how it must break their gentle souls to sell themselves and their hearts to survive. It was good for me to see all these contrasting aspects of people's lives.

I did support my rickshaw driver as much as I could, however, only to the limits that I could afford as a student having side jobs. We talked about various topics, and I was reminded once again how blessed I was. In my heart, I was dreaming about the day when I would be able to support these people even more. I was dreaming about schools I wanted to establish in the developing countries and about centers for supporting parents to create a better life. Yet my soul reminded me that these, too, are valuable lessons, and with my limited human perspective, I am not the one to judge it.

The next day, my rickshaw driver took me to the main temple of Angkor Wat. From the first sight, I knew that I had been there before. I knew this temple intimately from somewhere without ever reading a single word about it. I visited the temple in my style - slowly and meditatively. My poor rickshaw driver had to wait for me almost the whole day. Although I had told him that while I was in the temple, he could have had some side business. I would not have minded waiting for him because I was not in a hurry. However, he did not take that opportunity, and with a broad smile, he informed me that he was happy to wait for me.

My legs carried me at a slow pace while my hands were busy with taking plenty of pictures of the engravings on the walls. Since I have always been fascinated by the language of symbols, glyphs, and ancient paintings, I could read the hidden meanings of the carvings on the wall like an open book. They made more sense to me than modern art. The stories on the walls came alive as I was stroking the walls with my index finger. When I came across an old language that I could not read, I closed my eyes and felt the energy of the message.

The Light Language, as I like to call it, is a universal language. It contains more elaborate information than our ears or eyes can capture. The sound of frequencies and the intelligence that light carries are not unknown to humans. Many ancient sites across the globe encoded information in the Light Language. Currently, only a few can read it, but everyone can learn it when their consciousness and respect for universal laws advance. Light Language is our natural way to communicate that we had long forgotten. Our modern technology is trying to substitute the natural abilities which we call psychic. Throughout our immemorial walk on this planet, we have put veils over our perceptions and abilities. Although we have never lost our natural gifts, we have forgotten how to tap into them. Already as a child, I knew that in our times, more people would regain access to our ancient memories. The access is perfectly hidden in the safest place – our sacred heart. It is our responsibility to remember who we are and to see our past correctly - the way it happened, not the way we have been taught.

For me, Light Language is the most natural fashion to receive information. It allows me to see the past and future, as well as the hidden beliefs that lead to what we call karma. It is like looking through someone so thoroughly that nothing remains hidden. Even if they believe something to be true, the Light Language informs me that it is their ego telling them that. But in their hearts, they know that it is not true. Even though I have always been able to read the depths of people's minds and hearts, I had not yet dared to tell others what information I received. I was worried about being labeled weird at best. My inner guidance told me to keep it secret until the right moment comes. And the time came when I put my feet on the Chinese soil.

After a couple of hours, I was still transfixed by the temple of Angor Wat as if I anticipated a miracle. When I was walking through the last section of the temple, I noticed a group of Khmer monks. Khmers are a Southeast ethnic group, and most of them live in Cambodia. They mainly practice their own unique style of Buddhism. It is easy to spot them because the Khmer monks wear a bright orange garment hanging over one shoulder. My heart was beating fast when I was in their presence, but I did not want them to notice it, so I pretended that everything was okay. Then suddenly, one of the monks smiled at me and waved his hand to indicate me to follow him. Of course, I did not hesitate for a split second and was pursuing him toward the peak of one of the stupas with a little shrine on the top. We were climbing up the stairs in complete silence and meditative motion. When we walked in the sanctuary, he pointed at a stone where I could sit. No words were needed.

The monk chose to sit in the front, and we were both facing the sun. I was uncertain what we were doing, but I loved the mystery. A few moments later, two other monks joined us, and then it began. The chief monk whispered a prayer, then we all bowed to the ground, and we started to meditate. They must have had a tape recorder with them, even though I never saw it, I could hear one word resonating in the air – samsara. Samsara was echoing all around us as the sun began to set while its beams were caressing my closed eyelids. "Samasaaaaaraaaa," and I was disappearing into the bottomless landscapes of my inner being. To this day, I do not dare to say how long the meditation took, but my aching buttocks thought it must have been at least two hours. But in truth, it was probably a one-hour meditation that the Buddhist monks practice each evening.

After the meditation, I realized that I was one of the last tourists left in the temple area, so it was time to leave. After all, I received what I unconsciously came for. As I was crossing the bridge leading out of the temple, I smiled and greeted my driver, and we headed back to the hostel. On the way, he warned me not to leave my room after dark. Well, I agreed, but I was curious, so I went to explore the little town anyway. Most of the streets were dirt roads, but some with more traffic were asphalted. After a long search, I found a restaurant that also served vegetarian food. When I looked around myself, I noticed that I was the only single person in the restaurant. I was already used to not meeting single ladies on my travels back then. But, in all honesty, I preferred to travel alone because it enabled me to connect with the places in a way that would be otherwise impossible. I also did not have to solve any travel details with anyone, and I could only take my backpack and go. There was such freedom in traveling alone. The moonlight was glittering in the air, and I felt peace and sincere gratitude for another day well-spent, which also happened to be Valentine's Day.

The next day I continued to explore the rest of the temples. Even though I had charged my camera the whole night, the battery was empty when I arrived. The only recording device I had was an old mobile phone. Thus I gave up the idea of capturing the moments, and instead, I allowed myself to be awakened utterly to the charming presence around me. When I was walking between the temples, I deliberately got off the track and then spotted a wooden house that seemed to belong to some fairy-tale. Children were laughing and running around the house, and big white wild geese proudly lifted their necks as high as they could while fluttering their wings. It was magical; I stood there for a long time, soaking it all in.

My heart was also touched while I was crossing on a wooden bridge alone – without other tourists. Suddenly, out of thin air, hundreds of dragonflies appeared and surrounded me. It was like swimming in a sea filled with these beautiful dragon creatures. They reminded me of my childhood when a dragonfly would always come to sit near me or even on my shoulder. In some way, we were connected, and for me, dragonflies would ever be a prophecy of good times ahead.

The sacred area of Angor Wat has plenty of old trees with massive trunks. I would soak in their stateliness and wisdom. They would whisper to me their stories and the ancient times they remembered. Although I have visited many places, there have been only a few that I immediately knew that I would once return to. Angor Wat was undoubtedly one of them.

CHAPTER 25

THE INVISIBLE WAYS OF LIFE

A piece of puzzle unfolds in front of our eyes.
How can anyone know the mysterious life?
All our beliefs are nothing but lies,
Skyrocketing our egos into incredible highs.

Our illusions are magnified
While the invisible ways of life play their hide and seek.
We shall wait for the truth to be demystified,
Until then, our vision is weak.

The universe has its mysterious ways,
Be wise, and do not argue with them.
We shall never escape the divine plays,
But we can uncover their unique gem.

The next day, I flew back to China, but I knew that this
journey had changed me for good. Still, many years later, I
would recall my adventures and feel a wave of love,
childlike excitement, and peace flooding into my heart. The
energy of Angkor Wat has created a sacred space within me
that later served as a bottomless well of joy and tenderness.

Thanks to Greg, I opened my heart for human love once
again, but this time it was for good. Greg, as a great teacher
of mine, has taught me that we can walk on this planet with
an open heart and without fearing anything. As long as we
stay vulnerable and honest, there is no real harm from the

outside. The only pain we endure is the one that comes from within. With Greg's help, I set myself free because I realized that it does not matter if someone loves us back. It only matters that we love. We do not need to make our love dependent on anything outside ourselves. Having an open heart, no matter what, is one of the greatest gifts. It connects us with our divine self.

One night after my arrival, I was wondering about the invisible ways of life. Before I met Kahl, I did not feel alive for many years. Slowly, since I went to grammar school, I could feel the expanding of the distance between my soul and me. The more I turned my sight away from my heart, and I forgot the beautiful visions that I once had, the more disconnected I felt. Then when I met Luke, I was already long lost. I lost myself in the expectations of others and ran far away from my true self. Years were passing by in similar motions that many years later, feel like one long blurred dream. My days were monotonous and unfulfilling because I had given up on myself and on life. Instead of living, I was surviving.

Then I met Kahl, and an intense inner transformation sparked. Since the beginning, I knew that there was no turning back. However, it still took a few years for my mind to embrace this fact wholly. One moment – one encounter and my life took on another trajectory than the one that had seemed to be my destiny. But during that transformational process, I stopped believing in romantic love. The last thing I wanted was to think about loving someone again and letting someone near me. Although the high walls around my heart protected me, they also caused me a lot of pain.

But life does not ask us whether we are ready; it continues to flow. And that is good because are we ever prepared for something new that scares us? I was not. At least that was what I used to feel, but after countless divine interventions that my mind could not comprehend, I have given up the idea that I could see the bigger picture. Through various serendipities, life brought Greg into my life, and my heart could nothing but open. I slowly began playing with the idea that there are other men in the world than Kahl. With every baby step, I grew more comfortable with the idea that I could open my heart for someone else. Or even better, I could open my heart for me. I knew that I had to release Kahl from my mind for good. But then I had to open myself to the idea that perhaps my romantic life was not over yet. Maybe it was just beginning.

Greg had a positive healing impact on my life. Without knowing it at that moment, we were healing each other. He was guiding me out of my mind into my heart even more than I had ever been able to. And I invited him to the world of spirit, and through endless conversations over the well-known black Fujian tea, we discussed all the matters between heaven and earth. Our meeting also marked a new phase in his life. Greg began to open up to the spiritual gifts that he now pursues wholeheartedly as his life calling.

In some miraculous way, that maybe even he was not aware of, he managed to help me regain full trust in both men and romantic love. At first, I was trying to push him away, but as he was oblivious of my efforts, it soon became apparent that his love was stronger than my ego. With him, I learned how to be present in relationships and how not have expectations and projections about the future. This was highly liberating. We both knew that I was going back home in the summer and that we might not see each other again. Thus we could be entirely ourselves, without expectations. And I finally understood the beauty of emotional freedom in relationships.

I knew that he did not belong to me – a man like him can only belong to himself. And that was something that I learned could also be true for me in a relationship. We just were. Talking, smiling, swimming in the sea, eating delicious foods, having massages, and riding a motorbike. I felt very close to him, and I welcomed his masculine healing energy.

We both felt that he was preparing me for another period of my life that was to unfold later. He is one of my soulmates that I had the pleasure of meeting in person. In China, I learned that the connection with soulmates goes beyond the ego. The spiritual and emotional intimacy is healing and joyful. It is like two souls singing the same song in their hearts. Since I had met a couple of my soulmates, I realized that the more I became my authentic and childlike self, the better they could find me. Although we might not meet our soulmate, when we do, we should listen carefully because something important is unfolding in our lives. We receive the gift of pure love from our soul family. Meeting your soulmate is always a sign to collaborate with the universe even more.

With each of my soulmates, I could recognize their spiritual signature from the beginning. And it was always mutual. Soulmate connections, I believe, are shared forever. The more we grow internally and connect with our soul, the higher are the chances that we encounter our soulmate.

Greg prepared me for love that was yet to come into my life.

CHAPTER 26

THE ENCOUNTER WITH MY SOUL

For a thousand years, I whispered your name.
Covered by a ruby veil, I searched for you far and wide.
Yet in the depths of my cells, I incessantly felt your flame
While you patiently waited for me to oust my pride.

Drearily wandering in the valley of my fears,
I listened to the moans of my ego.
A shaggy moss grew through my ears,
Hence all I could hear were the murmurs of the foe.

In the darkest of hours, I remembered my soul.
All the ages shrank in one to help me to mature.
Ergo my soul can guide my path to the sole goal
Of embodying my essence and let it omnipresently pour.

It was Friday afternoon, and I was coming home from the extra private Chinese language classes that I had recently started taking. The sun was high in the sky, and the air was surprisingly warm for winter. As it became my routine, I had prepared a vegan lunch box with me and went to eat it to a far-reaching park surrounded by a river on the southern side. I found a tree and leaned my back against its mighty trunk. After I finished my lunch, I pulled my Kindle out from my bag and began to read. My eyes sunk onto the page, but my mind was chattering about something else. Once again, the same dilemma emerged on my mind, "I want to heal entirely, but sometimes I still feel caught up in between the two worlds."

At that moment, something cracked in me, and with all the conviction, I whispered, "Please, soul, I know you can hear me. All my solutions are moving in circles. The truth is that I have no idea how I can heal completely by myself. Please, if you can hear me, heal me. I do not care what you want me to do and who you want me to become. I will be anything just, please, help me heal. I surrender to you. I surrender. I surrender."

Surrender is like forgiveness; you cannot force it. One day it simply comes. Although I had tried to surrender dozens of times before, it never worked because I used to surrender with my mind. I made the decision and spoke the right words. Yet those words lacked any deeper substance, and thus they only resonated in my mind. However, that afternoon, it was different. The months of opening up my heart built a bridge to reach my soul. Under that tree, I surrendered with my heart. Only then, my soul could finalize the bridge between us. Only that day, I could finally surrender.

In that sacred moment, I surrendered all my solutions to my soul and God. It did not matter to me what I needed to change; I would do anything that my soul asked me to do. I craved to let go of my past entirely. For the first time, I admitted to myself that the solutions that my mind was offering to me were not enough. They would work for the majority of my doubts and fears, but there were still a couple of issues that I did not know how to heal. Despite all the healing I did, sometimes, I would once again wander in circles.

In that divine instant of complete openness, I allowed myself to accept the fact that I was here to guide others on their journeys. It was somewhere there under the mighty tree in southeast Asia where I, for the first time, allowed myself to admit what had always been obvious. I was not meant to become a business consultant, but a spiritual consultant for people who also have suffered, and now they want to find their inner light. For people who were, too, walking in circles and were now ready to find their true selves. As I kept crying, the illusions of who I should become were lifting from my mind. One after another, my false beliefs were transmuting to the light, and I was feeling peacefully empty and yet fulfilled in a new unknown way.

This was the instant when I began to communicate with my soul, consciously. I was prepared to do the work and show up for my life purpose. From that moment on, I was able to get myself into space where I could reach and hear my soul, as well as many other spiritual guides and beings, at will. The veil had thinned. I could now talk with my soul, just like with anyone else. For that, I did not need to lit a candle and meditate - I only needed to descend into my heart. I realized that I had carried the most precious source of love inside me the whole time. I did not need Kahl or anyone else to feel love and be loved.

For once and for good, I was ready to let my soul lead the path. I was tired of trying to figure out life. At last, I was willing to listen. I kept my eyes closed for as long as I could. I had never felt so peacefully empty as that afternoon. When there was nothing left inside, I heard the sentence, "Embody your soul." Electricity ran through the top of my head down to my feet. In my mind, I kept repeating these three words, and although I had never heard them before, I knew that this was my mission.

Still, with my eyes closed, I saw a vision of my soul hovering above the top of my head, and then a luminous light entered my body. As the bright light settled in my body, my cells were rewired to a higher frequency. I understood how carrying the Light of the Soul in a physical body can transform one's life. First, the body adjusts and clears out disharmonic energies, and then the mind begins to heal by releasing fear-based beliefs. During this process, the mental, energetic, emotional, and physical levels align with the Light of the Soul. Then there is only one step left – to embody our true essence in daily life.

In the vision, I could see that allowing the Light of the Soul to penetrate every area of life is a process that might not be accomplished in one lifetime. To inspire me, my soul revealed to me that my words would have a healing effect on others one day. I could see how my future choices reflecting love and courage would entirely change my life. I also saw my future relationship founded on equality and deep soul resonance. Instantly, I sensed that embodying one's soul is a process that leads to self-mastery.

Although I knew this was going to be a challenging path to walk, nothing else could satisfy me anymore. There was nothing I could possibly want more than letting my soul take over my life because it would create the most beautiful version of myself. Even taking a few baby steps toward embodying my soul would lead to massive changes in my life. After receiving this vision, a wave of gratitude and relief took over me, and once again, I knew that my life would not be the same as it had been. I took a chance of my newly found connection with my soul and asked her to help me understand the purpose of Kahl in my life.

The answer came immediately. I could clearly hear sentences and see images with my eyes open. My soul told me that Kahl and I have been searching for each other for lifetimes. Sometimes we came closer to enhance each other's evolution, and then we bounced off like two magnets repelling each other. The dance of pulling and repelling has created intense energy that has goaded me to grow faster. In each lifetime, we circled around each other. We observed each other. And those few lifetimes when did come closer, our interaction sparked atomic energy, the ripples of which could be felt by many.

The answers brought me peace because, unlike the twin flame theories, my soul did not tell me that we needed to be together or that I first had to become perfect to unite with him. I could imagine my life without him, and somewhere within, I sensed that it would also be easier that way. Although Kahl's presence pushed me to grow beyond measures, it also created energy that destabilized me. I could choose any life path even beyond the one I had selected for this lifetime. It brought me relief to know that there was nothing I must be, but I could choose anything even beyond what I could imagine.

As I was diving deeper into the connection with my soul, I received another vision. This time, I saw myself speaking on a stage, and I could see how the energy of my audience was shifting and healing. This is what mattered. Not how I could get there, but the impact I could create. I could sense that if Kahl were by my side, I would learn to keep his fears from taking me off balance. But if Kahl was not there, I could still achieve anything. That day I made the choice of being independent of anything outside me. Although I had no idea how I was going to dedicate my life to shifting consciousness on this planet and guiding people to transform toward the most beautiful version of themselves, all I needed to do was to make the jump. And so I did.

When I was leaving the park, the world seemed brighter. I decided to follow the vision that my soul had sent me, and

I emptied myself of the ideas about how to get there. I was ready to liberate myself from everything that was holding me back.

CHAPTER 27

THE ARCHETYPES

The wounded child told me to cry,
The Saboteur added, do not even try!
The victim told me it would never change,
The prostitute asked what she can exchange.

The four companions chase one another,
They want to have some fun.
Yet, it is a vicious circle,
I would rather hide like a turtle.

The heroine, please, save me.
Let me join you in your endless glee
For I want to thrive!
I am breaking the light of the archetypes free.

As I was guided by my soul to dive deeper into my inner healing, I came across archetypes. Although I did not study archetypes extensively, the knowledge of those unconscious blueprints of the human psyche, helped me to identify some behaviors that I wanted to let go of. The archetypes represent our collective unconsciousness, and thus they set the tone for our instinctive behaviors and emotions.

The archetypes serve as collective predispositions for thought and emotional patterns that urge us to make instinctive decisions. When they mix with our personality, they acquire a specific flavor, which is the combination of these universal predispositions and our individual self. Until we activate them, they remain dormant. I wholly apprehended it when I activated my heroine archetype. The potential to of my heroine energy had been within me all along, but until I began making more courageous choices, this force had stayed latent.

From the beginning, I could also see that the archetypes work alongside the family patterns. We can find these unconscious blueprints of behavior described in fairy tales, myths, and legends. That is why the legends have survived for thousands of years and are still narrated to little children. Although I could not name it as archetypes back then, I loved reading about warriors or philosophers from the past because I knew that we carry the same potential inside us. When we unravel the dynamics of the critical moments of someone's life, we can tap into the like aptitude.

Depending on the person and their mission, people have about twelve major archetypes, of which four are shared by all humankind. The four common archetypes are a child, a victim, a saboteur, and a tramp. It did not take long for me to see when I let my inner saboteur or my victim run the show as they used to be my frequent companions. But the inner child was the very first archetype that I began to work with consciously. The child archetype can manifest itself in various forms, which are reflections of the significant dynamics of our childhood. It is common for the inner child to demonstrate itself as a wounded child.

The wounded child is the deeply buried aspect of us that had suffered emotional or physical pain while growing up. Since our psyche and sense of self are forming throughout those early years, those wounds often prevail into our adult years. Of course, when we are adults, we may not be aware of the wounded child except for some occasional moments when the suppressed pain suddenly emerges. The thing that most people do not realize is that the wounded self does not thoroughly recover without our active assistance. Most adults carry their wounded child archetype and unconsciously allow it to govern their decisions. Soon I could spot the wounded child in others whenever I saw two arguing adults because, in those moments, the inner child likes to show up.

The child archetype can also manifest as an abandoned child. People who were either born as orphans or were not accepted by their family may carry this archetype. Even though in my case, I had a family, the abandoned child archetype was something that I needed to heal as well. The positive side-effect of this archetype was that I became independent early on in my life and could develop my own way of thinking. But the abandoned child was still not my primary archetype.

Once I was willing to look past my old hurts, I recognized that the innocent child archetype resonated best with me. A person with the innocent child archetype stays close to the invisible world and can even see the energies and light beings. The innocent child also stays pure inside, no matter how challenging the circumstances may be. In my heart, I could never have given up on humanity and the goodness in others, although my words did not always reflect it because I was terrified to be called naïve. Having faith does not mean being blind or deaf. On the contrary, it is about seeing beyond the obvious. Admitting to myself who I was without the pain, brought me closer to my authentic self. When we try to fit in someplace, we do not belong; we create unnecessary challenges. But when we discover that our home lies within us, everything clicks in the right place. At that point, I only yearned to align with my true nature, whatever it meant.

Another common archetype is the victim. The blueprint of victim mentality has been passed from generation to generation. When we look at our history, no further explanation is required. One of the elemental characteristics of the victim is that they do not take responsibility for their lives. It is much easier to blame others, society, economy, or even weather for our misfortune. However, it takes growing up to become the captain of our own life. We may wait for someone to save us without even realizing it. It certainly was my case. I used to wait for someone to help me create the life I wanted until I realized that the whole time, I was waiting for myself. From that point on, I changed my perception of others and situations and was looking for ways to empower me rather than keep me imprisoned.

The third collective archetype is the tramp or, as some call it, the prostitute archetype. When you sell parts of yourself to obtain something else, you are like a tramp without your own home and integrity. The work environment is one of the places where the prostitute archetype is visible. The tramp – the prostitute - seeks approval at their job, and thus they often work overtime. Or they make appealing comments and always agree with their boss even though it goes against their true beliefs. Therefore they trade pieces of themselves to receive more money or recognition in return. Another characteristic behavior of the tramp is that they stay in wrong relationships and do not stand up for themselves and their value. The prostitute says words that do not have any meaning because they only long for attention, love, money, or recognition from others. They say and do anything to ensure acceptance, status, or love.

The last of the four basic archetypes is the saboteur. The

saboteur always gives up when they face an opportunity to stretch their limits. Or they sabotage their chance to create a happy relationship or their own fulfilling business. When the universe gives us a chance to grow, the saboteur promptly replies, "Oh, I am fine, I do not need anything" instead of acting on the possibility. Then they withdraw to their little world and justify for themselves why it would not have worked out anyway.

As I was contemplating my archetypes, I pulled out my journal and read my old notes: "I realized that often when I stepped out of my comfort zone, the saboteur took me back into my shelter, and then the victim assured me that it was going to stay like this for good. But the best party started when they invited the third guy – the wounded child. This was a successful recipe for never getting out of the negative mindset."

I quickly learned how to spot these four archetypes because they were like a broken gramophone record. No matter which one of them overshadowed my thoughts, the others rushed in to make it even worse. It was alarming to realize how many of my decisions were affected by fear rather than love and courage.

But the longer I thought about them, the more I could see the ways how to tap into their positive sides. My abandoned child wanted my nourishment, love, and appreciation. She wanted to get involved in something creative, to transform her wounds into art. The victim archetype was there to teach me how to fight for myself and my dreams. She wanted me to understand my worth and value. The victim begged me to stand up for myself in the moments of humiliation or violation of my boundaries - even when it was me who had violated them.

The prostitute taught me about integrity and conscience.

She motivated me to speak up for myself and acknowledge the power of my voice. The prostitute guided me to my inner truth, which should not be exchanged for anything. It did not matter whom I was talking with or how arduous it felt to speak my truth; it was still better than to sell parts of myself - of my soul, heart, and mind. By listening to my inner tramp, I could find an anchor in my life, which would not give in even for the biggest of waves.

Then there was my ever loud companion, the saboteur. In the past, I allowed my inner saboteur to make crucial decisions in my life. Although changes are good, not all of them were in alignment with my soul's purpose. I had to learn how to distinguish good from bad opportunities and then to commit myself to the good ones. I found out that the saboteur could warn me against missing out on great chances. So what I needed to learn was to examine my motives when I was afraid of acting on an opportunity. Was it really a chance that was not beneficial for me, or was it my inner saboteur guarding my heart against a potential failure?

In the light of these realizations, I began to ask myself, "Who will I listen to? Which aspects of the archetypes do I wish to support? What are these archetypes trying to communicate to me?" Once again, I felt like a baby learning to master her first steps. Self-esteem, respecting my inner boundaries, speaking my truth, and taking responsibility are the areas we should master while we are growing up. Ideally, we enter the adult world with a clarity of our own purpose and direction. This is what they should teach us in schools. We spend years in our education system memorizing unimportant and mostly twisted information, and yet no one teaches us how to take care of ourselves.

We become adults based on age, yet we are not ready to

face the real world out there mentally, emotionally, and spiritually. We do not have an idea of who we are and what we want. Instead, just like leaves, we are drifting in the air. Being an adult does not mean that we are wise and have all the answers. On the contrary, it takes a committed inner work to truly mature. Far too often, we choose to listen to magazines, politicians, and teachers at school instead of developing our personal power and strength. Every day, we invest much of our energy into someone else's agendas.

Although the connection with my soul was strong, I also needed to learn how to find my place in the world. In the realms of spirit, things made sense. But here, I needed to relearn some basic things like how to say my opinion and bring my dreams into reality even if everyone else was against it.

CHAPTER 28

GATEKEEPERS

Where did you hide?
Where did you go?
You are my part,
My stray soul.

The bells are ringing,
The crystal walls are clinging.
The porcelain was already rubbed up,
Now all is ready for you to show up.

You have been dearly missed,
I mourned like a dying swan,
But now, I want to be avidly kissed,
Bring me the new dawn.

Become part of me,
You are my mystery.
Everything is waiting for us to be reunited,
To become one soul full of light.

It was Thursday late afternoon when I was returning from my classes. I decided to jump off the bus six kilometers before my usual stop to walk back home along the shore. The air was fresh yet warm, and I could feel the spring coming. I inhaled deeply and enjoyed the waves cascading onto the beach to wash over my feet. To my surprise, there were only a few people in that part of the city, and I let the silence sink into my body. Before I approached the busier part of the beach, I lay down on the big scarf that I always carried with me for that purpose and closed my eyes. I wanted to recall some of the conversations that I had with Elo. He was a Mauritius healer whom I met twice during the last summer.

When I first met him, Elo wanted to be sure that I was "a good spirit," as he said it. Therefore he began our session by checking my energy body before even talking to me properly. Although I was surprised at this behavior, I agreed. After all, I did not know any other healers, so maybe it was common. As an explanation, he briefly shared with me that he had bad experiences with people harboring low spirits, and he wanted to make sure that I was not one of them. Elo told me to lie down on a table, and then he covered my whole body with a white piece of cloth. Then he placed a few crystals here and there and began to move his hands above me. I could not see what was happening since he told me to keep my eyes closed. Still, I could feel his movements as if he touched me, but I knew that he did not. In a while, my whole body was vibrating tremendously. I could feel every cell of my body and the most intense wave of pulsating energy in my head. It was far from pleasant, but I was determined to hold on.

Once he finished, he asked me to stand up and walk over to his table. In the middle of the table was an old compass. Then he asked me to place my left hand above the compass about the distance of two hands away from it. I kept my eyes closed at first, until his words interrupted me, "Wow, this is amazing, Sylvia. You are a mighty soul. Look what you are doing to the compass." I looked down and saw the needle of the compass swirling around at high speed. First,

I assumed that he was doing it somehow, but after a couple of minutes, I realized that it was me. "In my 30 years of experience as a healer, I have met only two people who could do this. You have a great destiny, Sylvia."

Unfortunately, Elo did not share with me much more about the whole experiment. But he told me that after my return from China, I should contact him, and he was going to teach me what he knew. Although I never contacted him afterward, our two long afternoons stayed in my mind. From my palms, he could read my past, even though I did not tell him anything about my life. Elo also said that one day people would pay me to come to their places to speak to them. Back then, it felt like a beautiful but utterly surreal dream.

From my conversation with Elo, my mind drifted to chakras. As my awareness of the energy flows in my body had increased, I learned to work with my chakras on my own. Allowing myself to understand chakras at my own pace was an essential part of my healing journey. Although I could study chakras from books or online, I chose to give myself the luxury of understanding them by myself. It always turned out to be a better approach for me.

Our chakras are energetic wardens of our bodies. Traditionally, the Hindu teachings speak about seven major energy centers, but nowadays, we can activate more than seven chakras. Already before China, I could sense more than seven chakras in and outside my body. I was contemplating on how chakras, the energy wheels spinning in our bodies, relate to some of my issues. Already for a couple of years, I knew that I did not feel grounded and safe on Earth. After connecting with my soul, I was guided to focus on the first three of them that are also called lower chakras. As with many other people who go through an accelerated spiritual awakening, my higher chakras worked well, but I lacked grounding in the lower chakras. For a long time, the idea of grounding myself scared me because it felt like I would get trapped in this dense reality. It felt that if I had connected with this reality, I would have died because the energy around Earth is too heavy.

In a perfect world, we develop the energies in our chakras gradually from the bottom up. First, we plant ourselves on Earth and in our family, just like trees expanding their roots. Then we practice what we had learned in our relationships, and lastly, we become comfortable with who we are and develop healthy confidence and love for ourselves. Only then, we have an impeccable foundation for connecting with the higher chakras, and together with them, we can also access the higher realms. In my case, the process went from the up to bottom. First, I developed the higher chakras as I was always open to the spirit world. While meeting Kahl, my heart, the fourth chakra awakened, and then it was time to make myself feel comfortable in the lower chakras too.

As I observed others, I realized that most people had stored pain in their lower energy centers because we have been hurt by wars, dramas, manipulation, lies, or financial problems. However, this, too, is the art of embodiment, and thus I decided to mother myself and take baby steps with the seemingly essential matters such as learning to belong or take care of myself.

By healing my relationships and money patterns, I began to balance my second chakra. The healing accelerated when I once again fell in love with creativity. I would draw with charcoal, write fantasy stories, or compose poems when I was little, but then I stopped for a couple of years. Later in China, I took Zhongguo Hua classes, which were art classes combining the Chinese ink, brush painting, and watercolor techniques. In my spare time, I started writing articles for my first blog or stories on my computer that I never published. Still, the mere act of creativity had unquestionable healing effects on my second chakra.

After healing my second chakra, two challenging chakras were left - the root and the third chakra. The root chakra is the first chakra according to the traditional teachings. However, it is not the first chakra according to my experience. It has a deep red color as the alpenglow of the sunset, and it is located at the base of the spine. It connects us with the Mother Earth and our origin. Muladhara, as it is also called, is the link between us and our family, tribe, and society. It provides us with roots so that we can grow like a healthy tree. However, if we belong to groups that may not want the best for us, we lose energy from our root chakra. We donate our precious life force to those groups, and thus we empower them. I knew that my root chakra was always weak, and I needed to focus on grounding myself to enhance my sense of belonging to this world.

As I was reconnecting with Gaia and my roots, layers of pain were washing over me. This is the thing about inner healing; we heal in layers until there is nothing but light. Sometimes I would think that I had already healed something, yet it returned in a different form. Planting myself back to Earth was a long process, but I knew that I should not hurry it. Just like flowers need time to grow, so we also need supportive space to root ourselves in our lives. Instinctively, I knew that I should be patient and gentle with my healing, and that eventually proved to be the fastest approach to take.

Then I had the third chakra, solar plexus, to heal. The

third chakra is our inner sun, for it has a bright yellow color that nourishes us from within. Solar plexus guards everything related to self, including self-love, confidence, and self-esteem. I knew that my inner sun was weakened because it was challenging for me to maintain my boundaries. As an empath, my energy would instantly merge with the energy field of another person, and it was not easy to keep the distance. As I was working on my third chakra, I soon recognized another pattern of mine. I would not stand up for myself when it mattered because I avoided having difficult conversations or going into conflict. On the surface, I would agree or not comment on something, but inside I was building up resentment toward people who seemed to push me into things that I disliked. My old self would try to avoid contact with those people at all costs without ever telling them why I disappeared from their lives.

As a baby learns to take her first tiny steps, I also started with essentials. When my friends proposed to meet with me, instead of saying yes to whatever time and place, I gave myself time to find what also worked for me. Likewise, I practiced turning my attention inward before I agreed with something to make sure that I did not say yes out of fear of being judged. Slowly, I began to care less about how my environment perceived me and focused more on nurturing my inner self. With those little steps, I started to feel at home within myself.

As I was lying on the beach, I decided to do an exercise to call back stray parts of my soul. My soul recently revealed to me that parts of the soul can separate when we experience a crisis or an intense, painful moment. It can happen in a nanosecond or over an extended period. Those separated parts stay locked in time until we retrieve them. My soul guided me to the places where part of my soul had split so I could bring them back. Soon, I noticed that I could feel whole and more balanced within me.

As the sun was about to set, I got up and continued walking along the beach. When I reached my favorite part of the beach, I saw kite surfers crossing the waters and their dark silhouettes contrasting against the red sky. As usual, I took a few photos to enlarge my extensive photo library, which I never share. At the end of the beach, there was a wooden path that continued around the rock cliff. The walk offers a spectacular view not just because the part of it leads you above the sea level, but also because there are massive dark stones that give you an impression that you are on a different planet.

CHAPTER 29

THE HEART CHAKRA

A beautiful flower dwells inside my chest,
A white, innocent lily,
Rekindling in my life a new zest,
Guiding me into my days gaily.

The green light radiates from the lily,
Weaving a gentle net stretching to my soul,
To God, the universe, and all the deity,
Back and forth to the North Pole.

Let it shine as bright as the morning star,
You are the real me, my pure being!
The demons and darkness shall be mar!
There shall be no more of a false seedling!

It did not take long before the heart chakra meditation became my favorite. Since my spiritual heart awakened after I met Kahl, the meditation helped me to direct the immense energy to heal my body and emotions. The color of the heart chakra is green, and it blossoms like a beautiful lotus flower right in the center of the chest. The heart chakra is the connecting space between the three lower chakras and the upper ones. Thus it serves as a meeting point with the divine and our soul. The awakened heart is the center of love, forgiveness, and integrated wisdom.

But among all the stunning attributes of the heart chakra,

one is the best – it is the center of unconditional love. Unconditional love is not just a nice theory, but as I found out myself, we can experience it while here on Earth. The first time I experienced unconditional love or the Source energy, was with Kahl. But as I moved to China, the sensations of this energy grew stronger until one day, I could feel it every day no matter what I did or with whom I spoke at that moment. For two years, my heart was overflowing with spiritual love. This radiant energy was like mercy because it gently helped me heal my past wounds.

After almost three long years of thinking mostly about Kahl, I started to feel ready for someone else. The previous year, I wrote down a list of qualities for the man that I would like to be with. When I was writing it, I realized that Kahl did not meet some of the essential requirements that mattered to me. Even with all the intensity that I felt for him, I knew that to allow someone to invoke hopes in me and then disappear was far from a self-loving behavior. I knew that I had closed some opportunities for us, but he did it too. Recently, I could not shake off an obvious thought, "Kahl knows your phone number, and if he really wanted to be with you, he would say something." Although during the last couple of months in China, he called me sometimes, and he even suggested that we could have a real chance, it still felt like nothing but empty promises. I needed him to act. After hearing too many hollow promises from others, I grew deaf to them. I could not ignore anymore that Kahl was too scared to commit, and I was too tired to wait for something that might never happen.

Then, there was Greg. He was like a joyful, fresh air that I so needed. My heart melted in his presence, and as much as I enjoyed each of our interactions, I knew that he was not available for the kind of relationship that I wanted. Thus, with him, I never allowed my mind to wander too much. I knew the rules of the game, and I recognized his purpose in my life. Still, he made me believe in love again. There could not have been a better person than him, but I desired something different.

An interesting thing happens when you begin to love yourself more. One day you wake up and realize that you do not allow a particular behavior from others anymore. Your sandglass is already full, and you need to take care of yourself. It happens naturally. Suddenly, you notice that you react differently to situations. When someone is upset, and they raise their voice, you recognize that it is their negative pattern speaking to you, and then you give yourself the most precious gift – you do not get involved. You give yourself the freedom to walk away and maintain your own inner sacred space. So, it did happen to me as well. Without seeing it coming, one day, I noticed that I was ready for someone entirely new. When I raised my standards and acknowledged my own worth, then the next natural step was to open up for a new possibility.

One evening I went for a walk when a wave of inspiration rushed over me. It was so overwhelming that I needed to stop. As I was gazing at the ocean, I told myself that I deserved to love and be loved. I deserved to have a happy relationship, precisely the way I wanted. I knew my standards, and I was open to meeting a man who would be courageous, independent, love traveling, and who could keep up with me flying above the clouds. I also wanted a man who had his own opinions and who would not take anything without filtering it through his own heart first. These were my non-negotiable requirements, and I knew that I would not settle for anything less. During my transformational journey, I was becoming that kind of person myself.

That evening, I promised myself that I would wait for the exact kind of man I longed for, and meanwhile, I would keep enjoying my own presence. After all that I had been through, I did not care when he would come. When you get clear on what you want, you have to count that it takes time for the universe to rearrange situations and people to bring you what you ask for. I was prepared to wait because I loved every second of being with myself so that it did not feel as waiting at all.

As my heart was opening to human love, I knew that I was done with the karmic relationships and friendships. I already knew very well that the karmic relationship is controlling, blaming, and it feels more like an ego game than love. After I left Luke, I realized that there are also soul connections. With soulmates, it is easy to stay authentic, open, and share everything from experiences to dreams. You know that you belong together, and there are no doubts for neither of you. With a soulmate, the shared life continuously expands, and I can become a more joyful, child-like, and creative version of me. No walls or masks can remain between soulmates for too long.

I also fathomed something obvious, but it had taken me a long time to grasp; when it hurts, it is not true love. It is our ego that gets hurt. During my meditations, I could feel the loving presence and the absolute ease with the man I invited to come. I started seeing him in my dreams, too. The scenes were changing, but he always stayed the same. I knew that one day, I would meet him.

I also learned that the heart chakra is the keeper of sacred relationships. We can experience our connections with others from the sacral chakra and solar plexus or uplift them

183

to the heart chakra. When we connect with our partner in our lower chakras, there is a lot of fighting, as opposed to the connections made through the heart chakra. I was committed to experiencing ease in my relationship, and I sensed that it was closer than I thought, but I had still some inner work to do.

CHAPTER 30

THE MIND WORK

You covered my eyes,
Infiltrated my mind.
All your words are nothing but lies,
You wished me to stay blind.

My failure is your success,
My tears are your laughter.
Your convictions carry nothing but distress,
Your lies bring no real answers.

Today I take back my power,
I reclaim my decisions.
You shall not drain my bladder,
My weapons are angelic legions.

Although I had never stayed consistent with my habits, meditation became my regular practice. Soon after, the yoga became another. I had been practicing yoga in Europe, but the yoga in China went much deeper in helping me to connect with my soul and understand my mind. I attended various types of yoga, and the Iyengar yoga soon became my most favorite. Our yoga teacher had turned a former Malaysian embassy into a beautiful yoga studio. It was close enough to reach, far enough to appear in a peaceful and mystical world. The high walls around the mansion forged a tranquil paradise. I adored every small detail of the place from the pond with fish in the front yard to the spacious old 19th-century style rooms combined with the Buddhist statues and pictures. This became my sanctuary, where I devoted myself to the mind-body-spirit practice.

Each Sunday, I practiced a three-hour class of Iyengar yoga with a friend of mine. However, I did not fall in love with the class immediately. When I took my first class, I wanted to give it up after the first twenty minutes. I had never experienced any physically more challenging exercises. Right in the beginning, I had to stay in a downward-facing dog for twenty minutes straight. My hands were shaking insanely, and it did not help that we spent twenty minutes also in all other positions throughout the three-hour class, including the headstands that I had never even tried before. Probably every half a minute, I thought that I could not continue, and I should run away. I was observing the Chinese yogis around me and wondered how come that they did not seem to mind the intensity of the training. Until I realized they were not all right either. They trusted our teacher and were devoted to her. They decided to stretch their limits and just do it. That realization brought me slight relief.

Our teacher, laoshi, as we say in Mandarin, was an incredible woman. Although she seemed to be at ease while standing on her head, once she opened up to us, we soon learned that there was a tough story and hard work behind this ease. She had worked herself up, and I admired her for that. Laoshi was the strictest teacher during our classes, but the most delightful person outside the yoga room and I honored her for her will-power.

When my body shook in the greatest of shivers, she walked over to me and told me to strengthen my muscles anyway. My immediate reaction was to oppose her because

I was trying, but my body simply could not do it. But she did not take my excuse, and she told me something that I never forgot, "I cannot, is only in your head." She said that I was exercising my mind, not the body. "If you calmed your mind down, the body relaxes too," she assured me. I did it, and to my surprise, it worked. My body stopped shaking, or at least it was trembling much less. That was the secret recipe for how to stay still in challenging positions for twenty minutes. With each yoga class, I gained mental strength too. Thanks to our laoshi, I realized that it did not serve me to think that something was challenging. Instead, I learned to find inner balance and reassure myself that any discomfort was merely in my mind.

Later, I started applying this simple piece of wisdom in other areas of my life. When I started taking the Chinese language classes, and I had moments of thinking that it was impossible to memorize a few thousand characters within just one year, I strengthened my mind. My new attitude brought me a fresh determination to design a life that would reflect my most authentic self. Suddenly, I recognized that I had all the power to change the tiniest aspects of my life, and I could also rethink my beliefs. Although the time before my departure from China was irrevocably approaching, I made quantum jumps each day. Everything spoke to me; I saw lessons in every encounter, in sports, classes, meditations, food, and in every Chinese character I practiced. This new life of mine was entirely alien to the one I had once lived. When the waters of my life were shaking, I retreated to my core, which could withstand any storm. This new dimension of my life brought me inner freedom and stability, which were two new aspects of life that I had yearned for.

One afternoon, I set off to the hills. It was Saturday, so I had a chance to take a break from my intensive Chinese studies and focus more on examining my thoughts. During the last two years, I had become more aware of the beliefs that were holding me back. I could see the invisible string of each belief trying to pull me back to my old life. The only difference was that now I was aware of it and was more than ready to let go of every single belief that did not serve me.

As usual, I sat down on the rock cliff to sort out my thoughts. For a couple of hours, I wrote down my thoughts about the mind and the ego in my journal, "There is a lot of confusion and misguidance around the concept of mind and the ego. People have primarily connected the ego with selfish people pursuing their narrow-minded goals at the expense of others. This, of course, is an example but not the only one. The narrow comprehension of the ego does not allow us to grasp its real function. The ego is a faulty perception of us, of others, and of the outer world. None of the things which the ego tells us is true. Nothing. Ever. Some people are claiming that the ego motivates us to deliver better results or to get the best out of us. Actually, it only stops us from doing it."

Suddenly, I could feel that my soul connected with me and started to send me more information, which I did my best to record. "The mind is a pure tool for communicating with God. Always remember that we share the mind with God. The mind is neutral, and it is not designed to create doubts, traumas, or other negative thoughts. The ego is a separate part of the mind, which only leads to creating illusions. It is like you would tie a veil tight around your eyes. Your vision becomes distorted, and one day, you forget that the veil is even there."

When I realized that we share our minds with God, my heart sang. Deep within, I recognized that it was true. The mind is neutral, so we do not have to fear it. I used to be afraid of the negative thoughts having power over me until I realized that they are mere thoughts, and I do not need to let them stop me. The negative thoughts are not real, even though they sometimes may look like that. However, the separated part of the mind brings also valuable lessons for our inner growth. It became apparent to me that we are meant to observe our thoughts and maintain our neutrality so that we learn from the lessons of our wounded self, and thus we can integrate them into our lives. We should use our minds creatively and make our thoughts work for our own benefit.

As I got lost in my own thoughts, I slipped away from the connection to my soul. I continued pondering about the ego and how it distorts our vision. Somehow, it felt strange that the ego would be a divine creation, although, in the end, everything - the good and evil shall return to neutrality. It comes back to its origin, God. I could not let go of the image that my soul had sent me. In my journal, I interpreted it the following manner, "The ego exists on this planet because, at some point in our history, we decided to restrict our understanding of our true nature. We decided to believe in separation, which made us worship other powers than God. Soon after, we began playing gods and got lost in our own game. The original mistake is the belief that we are separated from each other and from God." It may sound simple, and everyone nods their head in agreement, "But do people truly understand that we are all connected? And do they embody this knowledge?" I asked myself.

An instantaneous realization rushed over me; the unity of consciousness means that we see God in our lover and in our enemy. We recognize the same loving presence in animals and nature, as well as in ourselves and our work. There is only one consciousness that pulsates even through our dinner table or in the people who we think want to hurt us. When we do not understand that God is in everything, we do not see God at all. The illusion of being separate from a person who hurt me only sends me further into suffering and separation from God. It is the separation from God that pains us - not the person because the other person is me, too. Whenever we raise ourselves above others, we prove that we do not understand the game of life.

The ego limits and stops our minds from operating at its fullest capacity. Our default mode is love, wisdom, and peace. The ego can be interpreted as everything that prevents us from being free, playful, and powerful creators, but the ego can also teach us. The ego creates our fears, as well as the feelings of worthlessness, not being loved, confusion, despair, or depression. The ego also loves predictability, and I could see the ways it would love to lock me up in habitual thinking. Whenever we want to break free, it enhances its efforts to make us believe that we cannot change.

As I continued writing, more thoughts emerged. I comprehended that a long time ago, in our evolution, the ego was created to serve us to focus on this life so that we tap into our true strength again. But somewhere along the way, we got more and more captivated by the lies of the ego, and we started forgetting our divinity. What we call reality is not real. In fact, it is more like a dream. We dream about nightmares, and we surrender to them instead of waking up. It does not mean that something is wrong. In all the creation, everything is ultimately right - it cannot be otherwise. The whole of life is about inner growth. We are here to integrate our lessons into our daily life, and to realize our true nature. I think of us more like amazing and brave souls who are on an exciting odyssey, which is both beautifully breathtaking, and painfully limiting. Yet the ultimate goal has always been given – we are here to recognize our unlimited capacity to love. To become love. Under the worst of the circumstances. Is it not mastery? A beautiful masterpiece of the universal tapestry?

We are mere wanderers on the planet Earth, experiencing all the kingdoms of the human mind playing out their creations. Each of us inhabits their own world. Each of us believes that their way of perceiving this reality is the only correct one. Our world is woven from the fabrics of our minds. The mind emits frequencies that flow like golden threads in the space around us. With plenty of souls incarnated here, these golden threads are interacting with each other and leading us toward new creations. There is nothing real in what the human eye can see. Yet, at the same time, everything that stems out of divine love is real. The love that makes our hearts vibrate and open up to our true selves and to others. Love is the fabric of the universe. This is the only reality worth fighting for.

In my heart, I knew that we have never been separated from each other. When we use our words as poison, it is us who tastes it first. When we raise our hands against our neighbor, it is also us who die a bit at that moment. One of the greatest mysteries of life is that we are all interconnected. Our minds and hearts chatter with each other all the time. It is only our limited physical sight that observes the separate bodies, as it does not recognize the fact, which every newborn soul knows that we are all one. There is nothing that we can hide. With every single thought, emotion, and action, we send out fireworks of energies that anyone can feel. One day when we remember this fundamental nature of the universe, we will be able to choose actions that support each other instead of harming them.

I picked up my journal again and continued with my train of thought, "The ego knows that it does not exist in eternity. It only exists as long as we perceive time. There is no proof that time exists in the universe, we only assume that it does because we observe the changes, but what if time was an illusion too? What if we were captured in a time loop? The mind is timeless; it can travel to the past and future. The mind is like radio waves. It picks up a specific frequency and ignores the rest of the waves in the spectrum. The mind is tuned to a certain frequency, which is indicated by an artificial starting point A and ending point B. In that zone, we experience time, but if we removed these two illusionary points, we would see the entire spectrum. When the mind is unaware of the whole spectrum, then it believes that only the frequencies played between the points A and B are real."

Before I knew it, it was time to go for a run with one of my close friends. I grabbed my journal and the empty cup of jasmine tea, my favorite one, and ran back home to change my clothes.

CHAPTER 31

ADA

Your loving words still echo in my head,
I hear your laughter when I close my eyes.
Sometimes I wake up and forget that you are dead,
Happily flying up in the heavenly skies.

Your charm still permeates the air,
Bringing up sweet remembrance.
In the realms of eternity, we forever share,
Our souls dance together in the glow of the crescent.

If you were a fairy, Magic would be your name.
With the wand of alchemy, you touched my heart.
Your hands embedded my worries into a playful frame.
For you, life was nothing but a piece of fine art.

Ada, my second grandmother, was like a bright star, always radiating positivity and magnetism. Unfortunately, with my family, we did not visit her as many times as I wished, but each summer since I was six years old, I would spend two weeks with my grandparents in their summer cottage. This place, which was entirely hidden in the thick forests, was a haven where I could leave my stress and problems behind and enjoy my childhood. I only had beautiful memories connected with Ada and my grandfather, who introduced me to the piano when I was six. I still remember the very first day, when he sat me on his lap and taught me a simple song. Instantly, I became so ecstatic that I grabbed a booklet with traditional piano songs and forced him to teach me every single one of them. Then he sat in his armchair and listened to me playing. This was our little ritual every time I visited my grandparents. Ever since when I play the piano, I think of him.

Shortly before I left for China, I visited my grandparents as well. Saying goodbye would take about a half an hour if it ever went swiftly. I would almost leave and then return with tears in my eyes because I loved them so much. Parting with them was always arduous. I would return and hug them and kiss them, then stand in the doors and keep waving at my grandfather, who was sitting in his favorite armchair. When I was sixteen, he suffered a couple of strokes, and his sense of balance was weakened as a result. Thus he did not walk me to the front door anymore, but I would still come back to stroke his bald head and kiss him on his wrinkled forehead.

On my last visit, Ada told me that maybe we were not going to see each other again. I told her not to be silly and reassured her that we certainly were going to see each other. "You are full of life and health. Please, do not talk like this because there is no reason why you should not be here when I return. I want you to see me getting married and having children one day. You need to be part of this. Everyone loves you and needs you, so, please, wait for me," I whispered into her ear. This particular goodbye was even more challenging than the previous ones. When I left their apartment, at last, she was standing on the balcony waving at me, and I waved back. For a few days, I felt awkward about what Ada had said, but my departure for China was approaching, and I was busy arranging the last necessary things. Ada was one of the most energetic and charismatic women I have ever met, so logically there was no reason to worry.

But once again, I was surprised at the invisible ways of how the universe orchestrates our lives. Much later, when I had settled in Xiamen, I met a guy who was attending classes at the same language school. Every Friday afternoon, we exchanged a few sentences when we ran into each other, but we never spoke more than a few minutes before our private classes started at the same time. For some reason, I had a feeling that I should stay in contact with him, but I never created extra effort to do anything about it.

A few weeks after, I woke up on a Saturday morning and had a brilliant thought to organize my whole day based on what excited me the most. The logic was simple; I would only do what felt joyful without any to-do lists or schedules. After playing the piano in the morning, I decided that it was a good day to go to a beach. Alone, only me and a book. I left the apartment and jumped on a bus that was just leaving. As usual, the bus was so packed that I did not have to hold myself because there was nowhere to fall anyway. Suddenly, I heard someone calling my name. I did not turn my head at first because I assumed that it was unlikely that someone there would know my name.

Then I heard my name again, that time much louder. I turned my head, and there was Dan, the guy from the language school. "Hi Sylvia, what are you doing here?" he asked. "Hi Dan, I live here, and I am heading for the beach," I replied. He seemed surprised to meet me there just as much as I was. "Oh, I see," Dan said, "I have never been here before. For some strange reason, I had a feeling that I should come here and try the local coffee place, and now I am going back home," he explained. "Would you like to go to church with my friends and me tomorrow?" he asked unexpectedly.

To be honest, I had been in the church only as a tourist wandering in old historic cities in Europe. Besides that, I was singing in one local church a couple of times when I was little. Not because my singing was fantastic, it was far from it, but because the local priest liked me. Sometimes, she looked after me, and we played some board games in her apartment. But I assumed that this was not what Dan meant. I was pondering quickly in my head, "Well, it is Saturday, and I think that people go to church on Sundays." I did not want to start explaining to him in the overcrowded bus that I do not do these things. Instead, to my own surprise, I replied, "Maybe, I can think about it. Is there a church in Xiamen?" His face lighted up, and he gave me the address and took my phone number. Then he jumped off the bus, and I continued to the beach.

When I reached the beach, the sun was already high in the sky on that March day. I enjoyed reading my book, and I was thinking about parallel worlds and quantum shifts. That was the perfect relaxation I needed. The day went by fast, and in the evening, I decided to watch a movie. I rarely watched movies, but that day, it felt like an exciting end to my beautiful day. Although I cannot recall what the film was about, I remember that for about half an hour, I felt entirely peaceful within myself. My body was vibrating so much that I had to stop the movie, and I closed my eyes to enjoy that sensation. I knew that someone was standing right next to me, although I was not able to sense who it was. Their presence was calming, loving, and soothing.

When the sensation gradually melted away, I continued watching the movie and went to sleep. I slept like a baby until three am. Then I woke up with a strong urge to check my phone. This is something that I never do during the night. In fact, I do not usually check my phone after four o'clock in the afternoon. During the weekends and vacations, I do not even bother to charge it. Yet that night, the idea to check my phone felt consuming. I grabbed my phone, and sure enough, there was a message that read, "So, it is here. The grandmother is gone. Daddy."

I kept staring at the screen for a while, trying to comprehend what had happened. I was thinking about the words, "It is here. How can you write it like it was expected because at least I certainly did not expect Ada's death." I did not know what to do, so I decided that I would meditate and send love to my grandmother. I sat down on a bed, closed my eyes, and almost effortlessly memories started replacing one another. With my mind's eyes, I could view every beautiful moment I had had the honor to spend with her. Including the moments that I had not thought about for years or the moments when I was so little that I wonder how I could even recall them. They were all coming alive like a colorful movie. I sensed that Ada was near and, perhaps, she was viewing this movie with me. I could see everything to the smallest vivid detail with a precision that was far beyond my understanding. For instance, I could remember the smells, the feelings, the ladybug climbing a hem of grass, and the look in Ada's eyes. Simply everything. I could not control the movie; it was played to me. I could not stop it until I had revisited every memory connected with Ada.

An intense feeling of love and compassion conquered my heart. I was crying tears of sincere gratitude because I felt thankful for everything we had been privileged to share. The way I experienced her death was fundamental to me. I was faced with the death of someone so close and so loved. Someone I admired and thought that she was one of the most exceptional women I ever met. From my point of view, her death was sudden and unexpected. I sincerely believed that we would meet again when I returned. But she knew better the last day I saw her.

I was almost twelve thousand kilometers away, alone in the middle of the night. I had not known how I would react in the presence of death. When my other grandma Brona died, I was seventeen. I could feel the sorrow of my mom, and I could not stop crying and feeling like I should have prevented her death somehow. As if it would be in my power. But nobody can prevent death. That night, it was almost nine years later, and I could experience death through my own lenses, and it taught me a lot.

As I was sitting on the bed, I whispered, "Thank you, thank you, thank you" into the dark air. I did not have lights on because I wanted to feel the moment with my heart. There were no other thoughts on my mind than of the utmost gratitude for the honor to meet this amazing soul. Although we could have spent more time together, I knew that everything was the way it was supposed to be. I was blessing her and wishing her the best on her next journey. During that night, I was entirely present to the degree that I sensed every cell of my body and every dimension of love and gratitude within my heart. I also felt elated for her being on the other side, free from the restrictions of time and space.

I told her, "You do not need to worry about me. I am fine, and I am happy for you. You can continue your journey, and you do not have any ties here anymore. You are free to go into the Light." These words were escaping my lips naturally, and later, I realized that this is what some indigenous societies experience when they celebrate the death of their dear ones. They do not delve in self-pity for the words that they did not say when there was still time.

They do not grieve, not because they did not love, but because they loved so much that they want their beloved ones to be free as a bird. The heart has nothing to regret because it knows that life goes on beyond what we can see. Each soul has experienced eons of journeys, and we all come and go. Yet death does not change the fact that you love someone, and they love you. When we cannot see our beloved ones in their physical body, it does not entail that they have stopped existing. On the contrary, when a person dies, they become more of who they truly are – a free spirit. When we release a deceased person with love and gratitude, we liberate them to continue. We can also hold them stuck somewhere in between this and the other world. If we hold onto them, they cannot leave this plane entirely, and this might be less than loving if it is not in accordance with their soul's plan.

After two hours of sending my love to Ada, I lay down to get some rest. It was clear that I would not fall asleep anymore, but I wanted to stretch my body on the bed, at least. I was lying on my right side facing the closed window when suddenly, an ice-cold wind entered the room, and it was forming itself into a vortex. It was too real to be a result of my imagination. It felt like I was standing naked on a mountaintop in the middle of a snowstorm. I did not want to move too much because I was curious about what was happening. I could see various lights from violet to white in the dark room. Then this ice-cold vortex of air materialized into a human body, and it lay down right next to me. It was my grandmother. She held me in her arms, and I could feel her touch.

Although I could not hear her speaking, I knew that she was transmitting a message to me. She came to me not only to say goodbye but also to share her legacy. Intuitively, I sensed that she said that there are no ordinary moments in life. Even the seemingly least critical decisions and instants count. Life is an impressive mastery that consists of each of our thoughts, feelings, decisions, words, and everything we choose to fill our days with. From the way we cut an apple, let the water run down our hands while doing dishes, and to the way, we look at our neighbor. All those moments are recorded, and we only comprehend their importance after we die. If you pay close attention to each moment and treat it like the only time that exists, because it is the only time, then you transform your life like a magician transmuting lead into gold. Ada made me realize how much control and creativity we have in our approach to every instant. She also said that this is what counts at the end when the book of life is opened and reviewed. There are no big or small tasks. Everything has the same value because it is all an expression of us. Each moment is about how we experience it and what are our intentions behind our actions.

In the morning, I was happy that Dan had invited me to join him and his friends in the church. The timing was perfect. I put on my best clothes and prepared healthy breakfast, and then I stayed present with the taxi driver who was taking me to the church. I talked and smiled with him as if he was the only person in the world. I gave him the perfect gift – my presence, and at the same time, I received it too. As if by a miracle, I came to the church too early. Although, just a while ago, it had seemed that I was going to be late. There were no familiar faces, so I sat down and began to cry out of gratitude. I did not tell anyone about Ada. I did not want others to pity me because there was no reason for it. She gave me the gift of understanding how to approach every moment. As it showed up later, it was also Dan's birthday, and we had great fun at the local restaurant until late evening. Then I came home and wrote an article about Ada's legacy for my website, then I meditated, and went to sleep. I stayed completely present for the next couple of days. I had never experienced that level of presence in my life, and it was powerful. Somehow it shifted me. Not because I had wasted my time until that point, not at least since I came to China, but from there on, my life was filled with even more experiences and moments worth cherishing.

Two months later, history repeated itself with my grandfather. That night, I also felt an urge to check my phone, and I found a message about his death in the middle of the night. They were always together as a couple, as life companions, and it made sense that he followed her. I never saw them without each other, and I even never heard of such an occurrence – so close they always were.

After I read the message, I sat up to meditate and to express my gratitude for having spent time with him. Just like with Ada, I also viewed our memories together with my grandfather. When I was still sitting in the lotus position, an ice-cold vortex appeared, and I knew that he was with me in my room. This time I could not feel his touch, but I heard him as clear as he was standing next to me alive. His voice was much younger and joyful, and he said one sentence, "Syl, I like you very much." Tears were dripping down my face as I whispered back, "I love you, too."

Since that day, I have kept being in contact with both of them. The death is but an alteration of form. We leave our physical bodies to become free spirits, and after some time, we return to the school of life. These cycles will continue as long as we need these experiences for our growth.

CHAPTER 32

UNLOCKER

When I place my hands on your heart,
Layers of illusions peel off your mind,
And your divine essence takes back her part.
The treaty with higher realms is now signed.

A white rose blossoms in your eyes,
Blue diamonds glitter on your tongue,
Each of your hair turns wise.
The sparkle of your skin feels blissfully young.

Eons of Light before the time was born,
The eternity embedded us with the Holy Grail.
We entered a different world,
Since then, our steps wander in a shadowy dale.

The Unlocker holds the key
To the game of life and death.
Will you open up to me?
Let your lungs take in the divine breath.

As my heart chakra meditations grew stronger, I noticed an
unusual occurrence. Sometimes I would have a burning
feeling in my palms like they would set on fire. Often my
palms would beg me to place them on someone's heart
chakra. However, I only had this feeling with some people.
I did not act on that feeling because I could imagine their

surprised faces if I would ask them in the middle of a conversation, "Would you mind if I touched your heart chakra?" At times, this sensation almost got out of my control as if my palms were living their own life. The sensation usually would also come when I was alone in nature. Luckily, there, it was not a problem because I could place my palms on trees and stones as much as I wished.

Another phenomenon that I noticed was that not only were my meditations getting deeper, but when I meditated with someone else, they also experienced the same vastness within themselves. Soon people would come to me and ask me if I could teach them how to meditate. Without any experiences other than my own and teaching a handful of friends, I accepted. Even if it was their very first meditation or they were beginners, each of them would experience depth to the point of absolute inner stillness. It is the moment when we feel like we cease existing. The consciousness leaves our body, and it feels like we entered another realm somewhere far. For periods of time, we lose track of our personality, our body, and the space-time reality. We are nowhere, yet we are everywhere.

One day Greg asked me out for dinner, and then we decided to come to my place to meditate. We had never meditated together, and neither of us had high expectations. I guided us with a couple of sentences into meditation, and then we both simultaneously disappeared into one of those distant realms. I believe that the whole meditation took more than an hour, but our concept of time or ourselves stopped existing. When Greg opened his eyes, he was not fully present because it takes a while to return the consciousness entirely after intense meditations. Then he said, "Wow, that was something! It was so deep and peaceful. I have never experienced anything like this on my own." As we discussed our sensations, we realized that we had experienced the meditation in the same manner.

Because of several similar experiences, I began noticing that I could tune into the biofield that surrounds us. I could tap into it and communicate with it, as well as to do amazing energy work. Everything within and without is alive. I feel it best through my palms and my heart chakra but generally through the skin of my whole body. When we tap into this field consciously, we can create things that seem to be out of this reality.

One day, I joined my friends for lunch after school. As I was ordering my favorite dish of vegetarian Chinese dumplings, one man got my attention. I had never seen him, and yet he felt familiar. Often, I have an almost uncontrollable desire to come to a stranger and start a conversation. It always turned out later that there was a higher meaning behind my feeling and that they also felt like they knew me. However, I did not always follow my gut instinct to start a conversation with others. But that afternoon, my desire won me over, and I stepped closer to that man. He smiled at me sheepishly, and we got into a conversation about food – what better topic in a school canteen!

He was a professor who came to teach a few courses during the one-month summer semester. We exchanged contact details and met later that day. We discussed various topics, but we did not touch any spiritual subjects, which at that point, was unusual for me. As I soon discerned, he was a scientist and an exceptionally logical man. We hang out together a couple of more times, and his two friends also joined us.

On Monday, after we had spent an enjoyable weekend with him and his friends, he asked me whether I would join him for lunch. Since our schedules matched and we both had finished the classes for that day, I gladly accepted. We went into a restaurant, and as we were sitting there, the burning feeling in my palms came back. The sensation got overpowering, and since there were not many people around, I asked him whether I could touch his heart chakra. He asked me what chakras were because he had never heard about them. A scientist! I gave him a short explanation, and he agreed. I placed my left palm in the middle of his chest and felt my heart chakra cracking wide open. I closed my eyes and was focusing on my heart chakra for a while, and then I sensed that "it" was done, so I opened my eyes. I was surprised to see that he had tears at the corners of his eyes. Then he started talking in a bewildered way like a person who just experienced a shock. Suddenly, he wanted to leave, and soon we walked back to the campus and parted our ways.

I knew that something had happened, but I did not dare to say what. If I do not like one thing, then it is fueling assumptions, so I did my best to get this experience out of my mind before I would create stories around it. On my way home, I decided to take a walk by the beach. It was already dark, and I could see a few stars – five precisely – that is how many you could see from Xiamen at night. I was gazing at the stars when my thoughts were interrupted by my phone beeping. One message flooded in after another. I do not know how many messages I received that night, but I think it was around one hundred. It was him, the professor. At first, I attempted to reply, but as my eyes laid on the mobile screen, I realized what happened. It was not him writing me these messages, he was channeling. It could have been his higher self.

This was not the first, nor the last time something like

that occurred to me. I had many similar experiences of unlocking something in others, and they started channeling without even understanding what they were saying. In many cases, these people would only remember pieces of information later. Although they sensed that something extraordinary had happened, they did not fully comprehend what it was. Sometimes they would channel information for me that I had never heard before, and the messages were coming from much higher realms than ours. When they channeled, it was apparent that what they were saying could not have been created by the human mind. The same happened with the professor. Yet, this time, it was strikingly intense. To put it gently – he was channeling like crazy! And not just for that night but for three days straight before his departure for the US. Even more astonishing was the fact that a previous day, he did not even know what a chakra was, and know he was skillfully using terms like oversoul, spirit, dimensions, thought-forms, or higher mission.

We met the next day in a local coffee shop. One cup of coffee turned into a couple of hours, and for the most part, it was his monologue. He looked super energized, and although I was tired, he could continue forever. "I understand everything now. The meaning of life, why I am here, who you are, and what your purpose is. I can see everything with clarity. I had been sleeping whole life, and now I am finally awakened. You opened my heart with an energy transfer, and I have access to all the knowledge that I had not even realized to exist." When he was looking at me, his eyes were changed somehow. His look was incredibly piercing and focused so that he did not even turn his gaze away from me for a while. He spoke with such severity that I knew what he was saying was true.

"They sent me here to make sure you are fine, Sylvia. They have been looking after you, but they have also been worried about you." Naturally, I had to ask him who were "they." He replied, "They are from your planet, from our planet, and they care about you deeply. They have been sending many messengers to you, but you have not paid them much attention. Therefore, they had to send me." I let him continue talking, and I noticed compassion and love emanating through his eyes. I felt how deeply he, and they, cared for me. "You are very powerful, but you are not completely balanced yet. Sometimes, your human form takes you out of synch, and then you block the power that comes from within you."

Then he leaned closer and said, "You are an "Unlocker" of messages that people carry within themselves. There is a higher mission for you beyond this planet. You and a group of souls like you make the universal wheels spin. Everyone carries some message, just like I carry it for you right now, and you can unlock them. Some of these messages are meant for you, while many others are for the people who come to you or for the whole society. But you need to learn to stabilize your emotions and the human form. You do not need to worry about how you unlock people; it happens naturally in your presence. The only thing you need to take care of is you."

He continued talking for a long while, and I met him again in the morning before his departure. We had breakfast at the airport and talked for a few more hours. He was repeating that he was here to make sure that I was fine. After his departure, we were not in contact much. One day, many months later, I did not feel balanced when all of a sudden, I received a message from him. He was asking what had happened and said that he could feel that I was not fine.

He could feel it all the way across the world because the energy does not know any boundaries.

CHAPTER 33

LOVE

At dark starlit night,
Like the waves in the ocean,
My eyes glimpse a pure stardust light,
We forever flow in continuous motions.

In how many embodiments
Have we chased each other?
To capture the sparking fragments
Immersed in translucent amber?

There is no victory in running away.
My heart stayed wide open.
Yet my feet led me another way,
Among us lies the mysteries that never been spoken.

I have found what I was seeking,
Although I did not find it in your arms,
My heart's fire is blazing,
My life is now filled with charms.

Two years before I meet the professor, I started sensing the world from my heart rather than from my mind. This was entirely new to me. In my previous existence, I considered myself to be a logical thinker. After all, I have two master's degrees in business, and during my studies, I always belonged to the top ones in my peer group. But the moment

I put my feet on the Chinese ground, I was changed. It is hard to describe how exactly it felt. Perhaps, the best explanation would be to think of it as a computer program. You delete the old operating program and install a new upgraded version. My remarkable memory was gradually disappearing. I used to remember any numbers that I had ever seen – from the battle dates, phone numbers, to any random numbers. Simply I could not erase them from my memory. I would also remember conversations that happened years ago. Even with people I had met only once.

During my stay in China, I turned from an excessive thinker to a relaxed being. I had been overly in my masculine energy, which I had not realized before. The women I knew were relying on their mental strengths, hard work, or appearance. Just as I had relied on my mind. For this reason, I had pursued the life path that did not make me happy. Although, the world I had built up made sense but only for the reasoning mind. I used to be captured in the world of my own mind, and I had not questioned its illusions. People I knew were imprisoned in the same way. Thus we played the roles of victim and jailor mutually for each other.

China surely did plug me into my feminine side, and I have enjoyed it ever since. The way of the heart is subtler, you do not hear it shouting from the rooftops, but a loving woman has the power of millions. A feminine woman who has also balanced her masculine essence within her and lives in alignment with her inner values and integrity. She does not compromise what she believes because of anyone else. She is like a night flower that can feel the whole universe in her petals and draw in strength from the center of the earth through her roots. Nothing can beat the power of a person living from their heart because they would not allow any external conditions to influence them. She is her own master who skillfully combines the softness of her lips with the depth of her wisdom. I do believe that there is nothing more beautiful than a woman standing proudly in her feminine power and the man standing lovingly in his masculine essence.

My heart became my anchor and guide. On a Wednesday evening, when I was Skyping with my sister, she asked me about Kahl. It was a sensible question given how much she knew. "We are now more in contact again, and he is considering coming to visit me for a month or so," I replied. "Wow, that's a big change!" She exclaimed. "Yes, it is, but you know, I do not think he will come. It is almost like we would have gotten a second chance, which is both exciting and scary, but I do not think he will take that chance. I have started to believe that he will never be ready."

"Why do you think so?" she asked. "Well, I cannot know for sure that Kahl is not coming. It is only my feeling. I can sense that he is afraid of what would happen, and, unfortunately, I think that his fear will win him over again. As it always does. Although what he is saying sounds like a fairy tale. Like something I had been waiting for ages, but he will not make that jump," I said. Later my intuition was confirmed. Kahl did not come because he needed to get a new passport. At least, this was the official reason, but I knew that where there is a will, there is a way. But where there is fear, there is no way for love. That I knew too.

"And how do you feel about Kahl?" my sister continued. How could I possibly answer such a question? It took me a long time that felt like an eternity to come to terms with my feelings for Kahl. For an outsider, it might sound like I was a woman desperately in love. But that was never the case.

There was nothing desperate about the way I felt, but it was impossible to explain it to anyone who has not experienced something similar. The words could simply not describe the depth of the bond I felt with him. The question about my feelings for Kahl was one of the scariest and most complicated I ever had to answer. Not to anyone else but to myself. I needed to find inner peace and move on. Unlike with anyone else, I could not have stopped feeling the deep connection with Kahl. Even though I did all the energy exercises that I knew to cut off the cords between us, none of them worked. On the contrary, I noticed that whenever I was suppressing a thought about him, it felt like a black hole would open up in the middle of my chest. Each of my attempts to let him go for good had failed.

Whenever I wanted to close that door for good, someone came unexpectedly and said something like this, "Yesterday in my meditation, I received a vision of you being like two bright stars who are almost like one. You try to get close to each other so much that the whole universe starts to shake. It is an illusion that you are separated. At the soul and mind levels, you are connected. You cannot cut him off." Even Kathy once told me that she asked God to show her what real love was, and that night, she had a dream about Kahl and me, and she said, "It was clear in that dream that you two love each other with purity. But you have to clear out the pain between you. Otherwise, you will never be together."

The most curious thing was that what these souls were sharing with me felt right. It partially captured the magnitude of my feelings, but I was still looking for a way to get out of it. "What was the point of feeling all this without ever being together?" I asked myself countless times while praying to God to make me feel nothing to him.

I begged God to erase any memory of Kahl from my heart and soul.

Gradually, I learned to accept our bond and stay open to it. After I returned home, I began coaching more people, and some of them have experienced something similar. In time, I began to notice that this is how the universe opens our hearts to unconditional love and invites us to love ourselves. The world is changing, and old structures based on fear and false power are starting to shake in their foundations. It is now when the legions of lightworkers are called to do their work and lead others back to love and light. Because of Kahl, there is a doorway of powerful and healing love emanating from my heart. I know that even if I do not work with people, and I am alone by myself, my heart is open and beaming love, which helps to lighten up the world. Therefore, it became a blessing and part of my life.

There is nothing wrong with feeling love. Sometimes we think that if we cannot be with that person, we should not feel the way we do. This is not true. Love does not know boundaries nor labels. We are only unhappy when we do not allow ourselves to embrace our true feelings.

I BID MY FAREWELL TO YOU

I still taste the dampness of your lips on mine,
Your eyes impregnated me evermore.
Today, was the day when I was yours,
Tomorrow is not promised to us anymore.

I put on the golden garment of my essence,
I stood in front of you in my purity.
There is not a corner within the realms of my heart
That I would not have invited you to join.

As the morning breeze erases your fragrance from my lips,
So does the sun burn your name on my skin,
The moment that took an eternity is now covered in
forgetfulness,
While I quietly wipe the tears off my cheeks.

Childlike joy and lightness rushed through our bodies
And before I knew it, the dream was gone.
You slipped into my arms like a night butterfly,
And spread your wings and disappeared in the distance.

I let you glance the jewel of my soul,
While I was viewing its sparkling glint.
Today I stepped into the next level;
I let the path dissolve under the clatter of my horse's
hooves.

That which was before is no more,
A new path is emerging in front of me.

Me, the Highest Priestess of strength and love,
Now chanting a joyful song of tomorrow.

I released you from my arms
With the caress of my lips, I bid my farewell to you.
You have never been mine and never belonged to me,
I shall never attempt to restrict you.

This is the hardest and most exciting of all the lessons.
You are a mirror to my soul, my dear flame.
But I plant freedom into your arms,
You do not need to be anything and anyone to me.

Today I made my bed,
Next, to me, the dragon sword rests,
I raised it proudly above my head.
If you ever join me again, may the Universe bless our
steps.

I release you from all the pledges!
I liberate you from your promises!
You have already given me a new life!
I shall no longer for you strive!

CHAPTER 34

THE RESOLUTION

At the core of my being dwells my love for you.
You had held my hand long before I knew you.
We used to discuss long hours when I was a little girl,
Then the darkness drew me into a whirl.

It has been all merely about you.
My love for you has been put to the test,
And I closed my heart in fear of you,
Until you humbled me enough to awaken my best.

I have longed for you ever since I lost you.
The years without you were a never-ceasing nothingness.
Feeling that I was missing something precious was all I
knew,
But now my heart finally rests in peace and lovingness.

I bow my head in front of you.
A stream of apologies is escaping my lips,
For I had forgotten you.
Please, forgive me for my sins.

It is an unquestionably arduous task to know the ropes of
life. Especially when we are on a sacred journey of inner
transformation. Sometimes we tend to assume that we
know the answers and where life is taking us, when in fact,
we are far from the truth, and we do not even recognize it.

If I have learned one thing in my life, then it is that we never know anything. After a particular phase of our life comes to a closure, we may look at our past experiences and be blessed enough to see its purpose. Understanding the purpose is a key step to inner growth. It is the stepping stone to mastering our life lessons, which bring us closer to becoming an embodied soul.

These are the divine moments when the universe is merciful to our praying and humble heart, and we finally understand the lesson of what we had been experiencing. We can merely see small bits of the tapestry of life and then try our best to comprehend it with our current level of consciousness. But even then, the most truthful sentence we can say is repeating the wise words of Socrates: "I know that I know nothing."

Life only reveals to us what we need to understand to master the key lessons in life, and the rest stays a mystery. Our ego attempts to explain the world and why we suffer and what is righteous and what is not. Our souls purposely choose challenges and initiations to awaken us to our fullest potential. What may seem as unjust and wrong might be the exact lesson that someone needs to experience on the eternal journey of their inner evolution. The truth is that we observe everything merely from our limited perspective. And of course, the present lessons may not make sense. They do not have to because it is not our task to judge the ways of life.

The soul goes the distance to fulfill its mission and to shape us into a loving and compassionate person. If we need to experience hell to awaken our hearts, we surely will. There are no limits to the ever-present essence running through our veins and souls. Life puts us into severe tests of our faith and the capacity of our hearts multiple times during our lifetime. When we are amid such an initiation, it can be extremely confusing and painful. Before we arrive at the other end, we can foozle for long years and feel disconnected from one another, and from life.

I humbly attempt to describe something indescribable here - as most of the things between heaven and earth are. I do my best to share with you my heart and hope that I can awaken in you the energy that I feel right now, so it may help you understand a little bit about what you may have been through in your life. When I was younger, I heard that some prophets were tested in their faith. My mind was thinking, "It does not sound too great. I would not want that. Thank God that we are in the 21st century, so it does not happen anymore. And luckily, I am not a prophet."

Well, my mind was dreadfully amiss – as it often is because the loudest adviser of the mind is ego. Not that we are only tested, but we also go through a significant shift in our lives, which takes us from our ego and our limiting beliefs and helps us to step into our hearts and into our soul's purpose. Just as natives go through rites of passages and initiations, so do we. It has nothing to do with religion and belief or being a prophet. It is an impersonal process and the way the life energy flows through us. Everyone is a student of life and always is in an apprenticeship. Even if we think that we have figured out everything and nothing remarkable is really happening in our life. There is still something greater taking place behind the scenes that directing our lives. But we are too close to ourselves and to our egos that we become blind to the larger truth.

My test was related to Kahl. As many people do, I also believed in twin flames. The theory sounds amazing. Especially if you meet someone who ignites the feeling of unconditional love in you. It literally smashes you. The magnitude of unconditional love is beyond the capacity of the mind, and all the words in the world lack depth to describe it. When I met Kahl, I knew nothing about love. All I was familiar with was the "ego love" when we think we love someone, but, in reality, we merely love the idea of being with them. When we do not love ourselves, we seek love everywhere. Usually, we first try to find it in another person. This was the case with Luke. I could feel his fascination with me and the way he looked at me. Since I did not love myself back then, this was the closest to feeling self-love that I could receive. I could see love reflected in my ex-boyfriend's eyes, and think, "Wow, maybe someone can really love me." Of course, this realization was taking place at more subtle levels, and I comprehended it entirely only years after we broke up. So there I was, experiencing the "ego love," and then out of the blue, Kahl came and provoked in me emotions of such magnitude that I had no idea how to handle them.

Despite my efforts to stay grounded and balanced for a couple of months, at some point, the mind came up with its own reasonings and explanations. Day by day, I was raising him on a pedestal until one day, I could not have reached him anymore. He was too high in the skies, and my mind convinced me that I could only have been happy in a partnership with him. I made him special and unreachable both at once. That was how my mind could explain my feelings of unconditional love. This distorted way of thinking made me believe that he must have been the source, and the only reason why my heart was set on fire toward the whole of life.

I believe that the twin flame theory is an answer of the ego to keep us stuck in the realms of being special. Although I believe we can meet a soul that touches us deeper than anyone else, the problem is in what the human mind does with it. I have learned the hard way that the moment we worship someone, we are out of the alignment with our soul and the universe. The twin flame theory is a master trap of the ego. At first sight, it seems innocent and pure. We have found our other half, and we feel divine love. But the problem lies in both parts of the sentence – we are already whole by ourselves, and therefore we do not have any other half. And the second part of the sentence was something that had taken me a long time to understand.

The entire time when I believed, consciously or not, in the twin flame theory, I felt disconnected from the universe. Not completely, but it was not the same unconstrained connection I used to feel when I was younger. Instinctively, I realized that something was not right, and I felt like being off the right track, but I did not know why. Until the test of my love and faith was over.

I was not tested in my love for Kahl. I was tested in my love for God. In my mind, I had violated the original essence of the universe, and I raised someone above my love for God. I made Kahl so special that I did not want to let him go. I wanted to keep him or if not him, then at least the idea of our love.

During this initiation through the fire, the unspoken question was, "Will you put that man, that relationship, that love, above your love for God?"

And I did. I did place him above God and then wondered why I felt such a chasm in my life. I had been in a long redemption that felt like an eternity. I had to become humble and pray from the bottom of my heart for a couple of years to be revealed the lesson I had been through. I was tested without realizing what the exact trial was. During that time, I was happy and contented on many levels. But there was this one topic that I was either avoiding or overanalyzing. It felt like stepping carefully around hot ashes. I was not completely present in my life because I did not know how to find peace with Kahl and the twin flame theory. Everything was fine except this one topic, which had been blocking my energy and leading me out of the present moment into illusions.

Unquestionably, this had impacted my relationship with God. I have always felt like the Source of life was my best friend. I have had a million discussions with God ever since I remember. My trust and love remained pure even in the hardest of moments. Until the time, I believed in the master illusion of special love. In the beginning, I did not see this change coming. I was praying and talking with God as I had always been. But at some point, I started noticing that my faith had weakened. A thin layer of resignation to life had settled in my heart.

My subconscious mind was playing the same song on a loop, telling me that there was a mistake in my life. The sentences I never dared to say out loud, but which were present in every cell of my body were, "What was the point of meeting the man of my life and feeling unconditional love for him when we could not be together? Not even for a week properly? And now what? How do you, God, want me to continue my life, uplifting others, and feeling love for them when I cannot be with the one I love? Do you want me to be like Mother Theresa in service to others and never to feel Kahl's love again? Do you want me to be selfless? Is that the task of this lifetime? If so, it does not sound so cool to me. I will do it if you want me to, but I will never be genuinely happy. And I am not sure if I can still trust you, God, after all this you put me through."

For years, this little poison was inconspicuously spreading in my heart – I feared to trust God again. Because if my trust only led me to this, I was afraid to open up my heart to the Source and invite him wholeheartedly as I once used to do. It was the fear of trusting God after he had "betrayed" me. My relationship with God had overflown to other areas of my life, and the whole time, I was wondering why I felt less in the flow.

Once I went hiking for a couple of days. And at least two or three whole days, I spent in silent prayer. My only prayer was to heal my heart and feel peace. About two days after the hike, I received the blessing of recognizing that I had been tested, and I also received information that now the test was over. At that moment, I sat down in tears and gratitude and apologies for my pride in believing that someone was more special than God, or anyone else. I felt deeply humbled, and my vision sharpened enough to finally allow me to see every detail related to my test. For long years, and in many painful ways, my love and faith in God was on trial. Now that it was over, it felt like a drop of truth and love from above slowly washed over my body. What my mind had been desperately striving to understand for years came at once in an eternal moment and shed light on everything.

We receive these blessings of clear vision when we ascend into our hearts, and we genuinely pray and surrender. It must be the kind of surrender that comes from the depths of our soul, and we mean it more than anything else in our life. In that instant, it is the only truth, "I know that I do not know anything. Please, forgive me for my pride in playing god. I surrender to you everything and everyone in my life because I truly do not know the way. I have been lost, and by myself, I am too little to see the way out. Please, show me the way, and I will follow."

The path of the heart is eons of years shorter than the one

of the mind. What takes lifetimes for the mind to learn, takes one brief moment for the heart. Yet we do not humble ourselves often enough to enter these passages that lead us to new phases of our lives. Although we think that we live in modern times, we still undergo the same transformations and initiations as our ancestors. Not every time we do recognize them, and even less often, we see the bigger picture behind the intentions of the life force flowing through us. Still, the inner transformation is happening for many of us, if not for all.

I had been tested in my faith in God, and as a result, things did not flow as smoothly as before. The test in that one area of my life had spread to the rest of it. This is the antithesis of life, we focus on our daily tasks and pursue our goals when, at the same time, it is, and it is not about them. It is about growing into a higher capacity of our hearts. Often we are short-sighted just like I was. I thought that perhaps because I was not good enough yet, other things in my life did not flow as freely as I wished. While the entire time, it was about the question of my faith and love for God. This one thing has penetrated everything else and impacted how my heart and mind functioned.

When the test was over, I realized how much I had missed my open, sharing, and loving relationship with God. As by magic, my overall trust in myself, my message to the world, in love, and in others returned and became stronger than ever. As if everything before was but a dream. And perhaps it was.

CHAPTER 35

I FOUND MYSELF

A little desire sparked in me.
To find my meaning,
To find the true me.
I set off on a voyage to the Middle Kingdom.

The Land of the Dragon spread its wings over my grieving
body,
So I could heal and behold the new world.
It was a blissful moment for me to embody,
I crossed the forbidden threshold.

A beautiful woman was born,
Full of light and hope.
There was a new moon
Swaying in the Dance of Life with the awakened globe.

The water accepted my prayers,
So I could merge with the water in one.
Diving deep into her layers,
The lesson of love was done.

After my graduation, I decided to stay and attend a short
summer semester at the university to deepen my studies
even further. We became a smaller group of students
because not many of us decided to stay for the intensive
month in July. We all worked hard because the love for the

Chinese language was our driving force. Before the summer semester began, two of my friends and I decided to go on a trip to the northern part of the Fujian province. Although the Wuyi mountain lies in the same region, it takes about nine hours to reach it by train. The distances in China are almost ungraspable for someone like me coming from a country that has fewer inhabitants than some of the Chinese cities alone. We agreed to hike and visit the famous tea plantations.

It was a late Friday afternoon when we were supposed to leave. I was wearing black flowing pants, a beautiful top, and a wide straw hat. I did not have to wait long to get a taxi to drive me to the railway station. While I was sitting in the back seat, the rays of the Sun were falling softly along my face. The Sun was fiery red. The ride took about one hour, and during these sixty minutes, I experienced something that I had been searching for all my life. My entire body was filled with a sensation of complete love and satisfaction with myself and whom I had become. There was not a single thing that I wanted to change. Finally, I felt whole.

I could feel unshakable love for myself and others, and I experienced a sudden epiphany of my pure potential. In front of my eyes, I witnessed fractions from my possible future timelines. My whole body vibrated, and I could feel my real strength. Not the false power that comes from the ego and yearns for attention but the real strength originating in my soul. I knew that my life purpose is to heal people's hearts and minds and guide them back to their most authentic selves. I could see how I can inspire others to wake them up to their true potential.

When you see into people's souls through all their masks, then you can heal their hearts. After all, we all want to be recognized for who we truly are. We want others to see our purity, our kindness, and love, buried under the layers of who we are not. Holding the sacred space for someone creates a powerful healing impact that can change them forever. Seeing people's souls has always been easy for me. Therefore, I did not have to think twice about whether this was something I wanted to devote my life to. Of course, it was. Nothing else could have made me feel more fulfilled than this.

Intriguingly, sometimes things come together effortlessly, and the most ordinary moment can turn into a perfect one. Once in a while, everything clicks together naturally. In that taxi, a new awareness of myself was birthed. I felt whole and complete as a woman as if someone would have washed off the past hurts and disappointments. My heart was wide open, and although I was aware of the past wounds, they did not restrict me anymore. I embraced it all – the fears, broken heart, and love. Which eventually led to the only possible result - love and presence. Whatever the future would bring me or whether I was to continue my journey alone, none of it mattered.

I saw the power of self-love as a sacred space in our hearts that roots us in the present moment. In that space, we are unaffected by the outside world and even the circumstances closest to us. For me, it was not only wishful thinking to embody my soul, but it also became my new way of living. Within the secret chambers of my heart, I found the sacred temple that could carry me through anything. There, in the least likely place to search for it, I tasted my true essence. Kahl was a tool of the Divine to direct my attention to my awakening heart. When I let go of the useless ideas of how things should be between us, I realized that I already had everything within myself.

The sacred heart is the temple where the human and divine selves unite. Our mind, our heart, and soul become whole and marry all the seemingly disturbing opposites into the oneness of life itself. As I was enjoying the ride to the railway station, I witnessed no more separation inside myself. I was not disconnected from God or my soul, and I knew that we are here to become spiritual humans – embodied souls.

Nothing is ever lower or higher when everything has returned to oneness. Everything simply is. Thus our body and our human self can rise to meet the soul, and our soul can descend to penetrate our hearts and minds. This bridge stretching from my awakened heart to my soul, has made that unity real. For me, this is Heaven on Earth. I was peacefully centered in my heart, and it overflowed with love for myself. This journey had never been about anyone else. Every single soul I met served as a reminder of the love that I had already carried within me. Therefore every encounter was holy because it allowed me to witness the loving presence in the center of my chest. In that sudden realization, I acknowledged that we all are love. We walk endless paths to comprehend that everything we have ever sought has always been hidden within us. It is upon us to awaken and embody that presence.

Because I loved myself, it did not matter what Kahl would do or not do. Or what others would think about me leaving behind the business career before I even fully embarked on it. I stopped caring about these little worries that the fear likes the dwell in. I became whole and complete, and I raised myself above this littleness that had dragged down my heart and mind. Although this state of bliss and satisfaction may not have continued, it was a solid foundation for the next chapters of my life.

At last, I knew that I found myself.

ABOUT THE AUTHOR

Sylvia Salow is a spiritual life coach, public speaker, and author. Her mission is to guide people to their true potential by embodying their souls. She helps people to step into their inner power and awaken their Higher Selves.

Salow supports people who are in the middle of personal transformation when their old world falls apart, and they are becoming a new – better version of themselves. She also guides Lightworkers - people who feel a strong call to help others through their spiritual gifts – to embrace their true power and do what they were born to do.

Salow has two master's degrees in business, but already during her studies, she began writing for well-known websites and coaching people all around the world.

Between 2012 and 2014, she lived in China, and this experience transformed her life. In 2017, Salow returned to Asia for another year, during which she gave her TEDx talk, and she was teaching workshops about the inner transformation, feminine power, and connecting with the soul.

To learn more about her work, you can visit her website: www.SylviaSalow.com or follow her on her social media accounts: @SylviaSalow.

You can also find her latest book, "Become the CEO of Your Mind," on Amazon.

Made in United States
North Haven, CT
07 March 2022

16908647R00137